D1411572

GRILLING AMERICA

RICK BROWNE

GRILLING AMERICA

ReganBooks

An Imprint of HarperCollins*Publishers*

All photographs by Rick Browne.

HarperCollins books may be purchased for educational, business, or sales promotional use. For information please write: Special Markets Department, HarperCollins Publishers Inc., 10 East 53rd Street, New York, NY 10022.

FIRST EDITION

Designed by Brenden Hitt

Illustrations on pages 148, 162, and 228 by Marsha Matta

Library of Congress Cataloging-in-Publication Data

Browne, Rick, 1946–
    Grilling America / Rick Browne.
        p. cm.
    Includes index.
    ISBN 0-06-052719-6
    1. Barbecue cookery—United States. I. Title.

  TX840.B3B7623 2003
  641.5'784—dc21   2002037122

03 04 05 06 07   QW   10 9 8 7 6 5 4 3 2 1

This book is dedicated to all the new friends I've made along the BBQ trail, the old friends who believed in me and encouraged my efforts, and, most especially, my family. A toast to Kathy, my wonderful life partner, and our children: Kara, Kevin, Tricia, and Christopher, who are all the brightest stars in my universe.

CONTENTS

INTRODUCTION
ThankQUE America

Is it barbecue or grilling? As he carefully sprays the cinder-black beef brisket, which he has been nurturing for thirty-two straight hours at 220°F, Brett says, "Barbecue can *only* be defined as the cooking of meat over low heat for long periods of time."

But Andy throws a misshapen burger on a hot grill over a 600 degree fire, sprinkles seasoned salt and steak sauce on it, flips it over once or twice, and happily calls that process "barbecue."

And you know what? They're both right.

"Slow and low" purists decry the speed with which grillers sear and serve their meat. "Grillers" don't have time to cook either slow or low. But Andy is just as happy munching his 5-minute burger on the back porch as Brett is savoring each bite of his buttery brisket after 1,920 minutes of cooking.

After all, the heating method, fuel, or barbecue equipment we use really don't matter a smidgen. The taste of the finished product, however, matters a whole lot. And it seems that just about everyone is barbecuing (er, grilling) these days. In fact, in families of four or more in the U.S. a whopping 91 percent now own outdoor cookers. People cook on gas grills, charcoal kettle cookers, electric grills, pellet and water smokers, deep fryers, and some even still use hardwood logs in their bullet smokers to slow-cook their grub.

Many families have more than one way to cook outdoors—it's estimated that a fifth of all grill owners have BOTH a gas and charcoal unit. And everywhere you look, sales of charcoal grills, gas grills, deep-fat propane-fired fryers, and even electric grills are skyrocketing.

But remember it's not what you cook on. It's **what** you cook, **how** you cook it, and most important, **how the results taste.** Whether you use natural gas, lump charcoal, propane, fruitwood logs, briquettes, grapevines, hardwood pellets, coconut shells, electric heating elements, nutshells, hot oil, or a combination of all of these, outdoor cooking is simply, as the name implies, using some sort of heat source outdoors.

It's no rocket science, Floyd. The same rules apply on the patio as in the kitchen. That $32 butterflied leg of lamb can be done just right inside or incinerated beyond recognition outside. Or vice versa.

You can prepare a soufflé on a gas grill just like you can in your $3,500 gas oven. You can reduce a perfect rib-eye steak to charred fibers on your charcoal grill just as easily as you can under the broiler of your old, reliable, never-fail kitchen stove.

What we hope to present here is a way to expand your outdoor grillery beyond hamburgers and hot dogs. And although dogs and burgers—and that good old standby, BBQ chicken—are still the mainstays of outdoor cooking, backyard cooks are attempting, and successfully undertaking, more creative culinary endeavors.

We'll show you how to barbecue ice cream. How to do things on your grill that chefs accomplish in fancy restaurants for $30 a plate. How to make your own "custom" BBQ sauce using commercially bottled "generic" sauces as a base. And how to dazzle visitors who come expecting fair backyard fare and instead get great grilling.

But mostly we hope to share with our readers how to have fun creating rhapsodies of smoke, spice, and fire on your lowly backyard barbecue grill.

It was interesting to learn during our travels that at some of the biggest barbecue contests in the country, where the most accomplished BBQ chefs in the world compete for $60,000 in prizes, that $29 hardware-store bullet smokers can hold their own against $30,000 custom-built, stainless-steel, computer-controlled, high-tech smokers that fill 32-foot trailers.

No judge, pitmaster, backyard critic, or even mother-in-law cares how the taste gets into the meat. The trick is to be damn sure it gets there!

For heaven's sake, be bold, broaden your Que quotient, and get out and experiment. If you live in North Carolina, try a California Tri-tip roast basted in olive oil, garlic, and balsamic vinegar. If you live in Maine, cedar-plank barbecue an Alaska Copper River salmon. And if you live in Vancouver, go ahead, cook Owensboro grilled lamb with Kentucky-style black dip.

Missouri grillers need to slop yellow mustard sauce from Georgia on their St. Louis ribs, at the same time that available bold pitmasters in Houston should go ahead and commit BBQ heresy by drizzling a Pacific Rim hoisin-soy sauce on their beloved brisket.

With so many regional styles of barbecue available, why cook with the same methods, sauces, or rubs that you've used for years? It's time for America to follow a few brave adventurers and break out of the barbecue doldrums. Time to Que something completely new, or grill something cherished and familiar in a brand-new way.

INTRODUCTION

Over two thousand bottled BBQ sauces are commercially available. Literally thousands of kinds of rubs are waiting to enhance anything you wish to rub them on. Once-rare regional food specialties are now readily available coast to coast. And folks just like us spent a whopping $845 million in barbecue restaurants last year. Frankly, it's a sin to isolate, ignore, or neglect educating your BBQ taste buds any longer.

Break free! Go for it! Grab this book—or any one of 100+ BBQ tomes written in the last five years—and boldly go where no man, or woman, has gone before. Close your eyes, open this book to just about any page, and try whatever is written there. *Youse got nuttin' to lose, Bub.*

We've tried our best to open up the barbecue scene for everyone to enjoy. We've grilled, smoked, BBQ-baked, fried, broiled, rotisseried, boiled, and braised whatever came our way. All in an attempt to put great-tasting food on your table. And we think you'll enjoy the process itself, as well as the diversity of tastes, styles, and methods we've set before you.

Grilling America, like its older brother, *Barbecue America,* hopes to share with you the best of the Que we've sampled in five years of travel across America's barbecue heartland, a heartland that has magically expanded to reach from sea to shining sea.

No longer is GREAT BARBECUE indigenous only south of the Mason-Dixon line. World-class pork ribs can be found in Seattle, Syracuse, or Sacramento. Today, whole hogs, once the exclusive domain of the Deep South, are barbecued in pits from Rockport, Maine, to Rock Port, Missouri, to Rockport, Washington.

Black as a meteorite and mouthwateringly tender Texas-style brisket can be enjoyed in Dallas (of course), but also in Detroit, Dayton, and Danbury. That's Michigan, Ohio, and Connecticut for the geographically challenged.

And genuine pulled pork-shoulder sandwiches topped with crisp, mustardy coleslaw are almost as easy to find north, east, and west of Dixie as they are in southern BBQ sanctuaries like Lexington, North Carolina, or Columbus, Georgia.

Barbecue is literally on fire across America.

All we ask is that you make the effort to try a new rub, sauce, and recipe as you join us in fanning the flames.

Rick Browne, Ph.B.

This Georgie Boy coach is my home on the road as we travel from coast to coast seeking America's best barbecue.

⋆(Indirect)⋆
GRILLING

Everyone knows how to grill a hamburger, hot dog, or steak. You take the meat, throw it on the hot barbecue grill, turn it once or twice so it doesn't burn (too much anyway), and then slap it on a plate, burger bun, or hot dog roll, and chow down.

WRONG!

Grilling is actually much more of a refined culinary art. Sure, you put what you're cooking on a hot grill, but the above method usually guarantees dry, tasteless meat that almost always has a charred surface somewhere. How many times have you hidden a charred burger or chicken breast with oodles of barbecue sauce, mustard, or ketchup?

A better way to grill is to use a combination of "direct grilling," as above, and "indirect grilling," cooking the food *away* from the heat source, slowly, thereby keeping it juicy, tender, and loaded with taste.

For those who cook with charcoal briquettes, mesquite chunks, or hickory logs: When putting these combustible materials into the barbecue, place them on *one side only* of the bottom of the barbecue. Leave the other half of the bottom empty (for now) and start your fire as you normally would, preferably with an electric firestarter or kindling, *not* flammable chemicals, which can then flavor (actually dis-flavor) the food you want to cook.

When the fuel is up to temperature (you know, covered with a thin film of white ash, etc.), take an old metal pan or a new aluminum foil pan that's about

The fountain of youth, next week's lottery numbers, and the cure for pattern baldness? Nope! Just the best way to grill just about everything from beer-butt to burgers.

9 × 12 inches and, using barbecue mitts, place the pan on the empty side of the grill bottom. Using a large pitcher, fill the pan with 1 to 2 inches of water.

Now place your grill rack over the coals. At this time you should probably clean and oil it, if you haven't already done so. Be careful not to burn yourself.

Some hints here: If you have an expensive copper grill brush, for heaven's sake, use it to scrape off the remains of your last BBQ immolation. But if you don't have such fancy gear, take a 12- × 12-inch piece of aluminum foil, wad it up loosely into a ball, and, using long tongs, use the foil to scrape off the grill after it's been over the fire for 2 to 3 minutes. The foil works wonders on getting the majority of the burned-on food off the grill rack, and you just discard it after using it. The hot fire will take care of the rest of the remains during the heating period.

Now sit back, close the lid on the barbecue, grab a brew, pull up a lounge chair, and relax until the fire is at the correct temperature for what you're cooking.

At this point you should "oil the grill." A good way to do this is to take a sheet of paper towel and fold it into a square measuring 2 × 2 inches (or similar). Again using long tongs, dip the paper towel into a small bowl of olive, vegetable, or other favorite cooking oil. Then rub it across the grill surface, covering the entire grill rack. You may have to redip the towel several times.

You could also keep one barbecue basting brush handy for just this purpose, dipping the brush into the oil, then brushing it across the rack. However,

if the bristles are plastic, you'll have a melted mass at the other end of the brush. Natural bristles last much longer.

Either the oiled towel or the brushed-on oil method works fine.

However, some adventurous folks like to use a nonstick spray, which they try to spray across the heated grill surface. NOPE! Not a good thing to do unless you really want a wall of flames shooting toward you! The aerosol spray can easily catch fire and, with a dramatic *whoosh* you've succeeded in barbe-cuing—your face!

Now that the grill is on the barbecue, and is well oiled, you can add the food you wish to Que.

I often start out placing the meat, poultry, fish, or veggies on the "hot" side of the grill. *(Remember, the coals, briquettes, or other fuels are only on one side of the barbecue.)* This way I can sear the food with a high heat, keeping the natural juices inside. Depending on the food, its thickness, and the fire temperature below, I'll cook the food for a short time on each side over the higher heat, 2 to 3 minutes on average.

Then, again depending on the recipe, I'll move the food to the "cool" side of the grill. (Cool is a relative term here: the "hot" side of the grill may be at 600° to 700°F, while the cool side may be as high as 400° to 500°F or there-abouts.)

The cool side of the grill, you remember, is also over the pan of water, which keeps flames from flaring up and engulfing the food, something that often happens when you just "direct grill." Fat drips onto the hot coals, flames shoot up, and you've got fire charring everything on the barbecue.

The water in the pan also evaporates during the cooking process, and the steam helps keep the food above it moist, juicy, and tasty. Note: some folks like to throw herbs, citrus slices, onion peels, etc., into the water to "flavor" the steam. I personally don't think this does anything other than give you a colorful pan of water, but if you wish, give it a try.

Presto, chango! now you're INDIRECT COOKING on charcoal (or wood or bri-quettes).

In a later chapter I'll discuss how to make this setup into a grill-smoker too, adding fragrant wood smoke to your indirectly grilled vittles (see page 250).

If you have a gas grill the process is much the same, only different. Most gas barbecues have two burners, some have three, and a few have four or more burners. Don't matter, as long as there are at least two.

9

Turn the flame on on only one burner. Place your water pan over the unlit burner and ta-da! you've got your gas grill set up. Because of the height of some burners you may have to put bricks on both sides of the unlit burner to balance the water pan. Easily done.

Clean and oil the rack the same way, and in the same sequence, as described with the charcoal barbecue, and you can cook your heart away. Well, not really, that would hurt a mite. First place the food on the hot side to sear, then on the cool side to cook for the rest of the time. Voilà! you're INDIRECT COOKING on gas.

If you've got more burners you can be a bit more creative. With a three-burner setup you can turn on both "outside" burners (to the same temperature, please; otherwise you'll cook one side of your grub quicker). Then place the water pan over the middle burner, therefore having even heat on both sides of what you're cookin'. Again, sear on the hot side and cook for the duration on the cool side.

Using this method you can virtually cook anything on a barbecue that you can cook in your kitchen oven. Remember that a barbecue is just a sort of outdoor oven. It has a heat source (gas, briquettes, or coals) like an oven (remember Granny's woodstove, Bub?), it's an enclosed box like an oven, and you can, somewhat anyway, control the heat like an oven.

Using INDIRECT COOKING I've made soufflés; baked bread, custards, cakes, and pies; and cooked perfectly what otherwise might have been incinerated over direct heat. And the slower, lower cooking temperature, after the meat has been seared to keep the juices inside, gives just about the best results possible to those expensive cuts of meat that you splurge on for special occasion barbecues.

As a novice barbecuer I sinned like many of you, making up all the excuses you've uttered yourselves: "That black crispiness? Oh, that's just a new blackened BBQ sauce technique I'm trying, honey." Or, "No, Chris, those aren't hockey pucks, they're Daddy's burgers, they'll taste fine, trust me." And of course: "This grill just doesn't work right, everything burns, here I turn my back for just the last quarter of the game, you know the 'Niners won, and the steaks look (gulp) burned."

It's okay, fellow Bubbaquers, now you can be "cool" and never, ever have to scrape the burned flesh from a burger, chicken wing, or T-bone again. Your steaks will be a perfect medium rare, your beer-butt birds golden and juicy, and your burgers . . . well it doesn't get much better!

HOW TO JUDGE BBQ GRILL TEMPERATURES WITHOUT A THERMOMETER

Following is a way to estimate grill temperature by holding your hand right over the BBQ grill surface. If you can only hold your hand 1 to 2 inches above the grill for 1 second, the temperature of the fire is approximately 600°F or higher. If you can hold it for 2 seconds, the temperature is between 500° and 650°F, and so forth. Please be careful not to burn yourself!

1 second (or less) = Very Hot Fire	(600°F or more)
2 seconds = Hot Fire	(500° to 650°F)
3 seconds = Medium-Hot Fire	(450° to 550°F)
4 seconds = Medium Fire	(400° to 500°F)
5 seconds = Low-Medium Fire	(300° to 400°F)
6 seconds (or more) = Very Low Fire	(300°F or less)

APPETIZERS

ARMADILLO EGGS

I serve these with very cold longneck beer.

12 medium jalapeño peppers

FILLING

½ cup Velveeta cheese
½ teaspoon garlic salt
¼ teaspoon McCormick Cajun seasoning
¼ teaspoon white or black pepper

1 large egg, beaten
½ pound ground chuck
½ teaspoon onion powder
½ teaspoon dried parsley
Pinch of tarragon
12 slices smoked bacon

Cut the jalapeños in half, seed them and fill with the Velveeta cheese and the spice mixture, then put them back together. Mix the egg into the ground beef, add the onion powder, parsley, and tarragon, and mold a small amount of the meat around each pepper. Wrap each burger-pepper with a slice of thick bacon, securing with toothpicks.

Cook on a grill-smoker alongside ribs or pork shoulder at 200°F for approximately 1 hour, or until the bacon crisps and the meat is browned.

Serves 4 to 6

14

FRICKLES / FRIED PICKLES

These deep-fried pickles make a great, if quite surprising, appetizer for any barbecue meal. Serve with icy cold beer in frosted mugs.

1 cup flour

1 cup yellow cornmeal

1 tablespoon McCormick barbecue seasoning

$\frac{1}{2}$ cup prepared mustard

$\frac{1}{8}$ cup beer

20 to 30 dill pickle slices

Combine the flour, cornmeal, and barbecue seasoning, and place in a medium bowl. Make a slurry of mustard and beer in a separate medium bowl.

Dip the pickle slices in the mustard mixture and then in the flour-cornmeal mix. Deep-fry at 325°F in peanut or canola oil until the batter is browned. The pickles will float to the top when done.

16

Serves 4 to 8

CB'S OH-YOU-DEVIL EGGS

6 extra-large eggs

$\frac{1}{2}$ teaspoon salt

$\frac{1}{8}$ teaspoon pepper

1 teaspoon sugar

1 teaspoon prepared mustard

1 teaspoon cider vinegar

3 tablespoons mayonnaise

Paprika

Place the eggs gently into a medium pan. Add cold water to $\frac{1}{2}$ inch above the tops of the eggs. Cover the pan and heat slowly to boiling, then im-

mediately turn the heat down to very low so the water is barely simmering. Cook for 20 minutes.

Place the pan in the sink and run it under cold water till cool enough to handle. Remove the eggs, tap them lightly all over, and then peel them under cold running water. Cut each egg in half lengthwise. Remove the yolks carefully, putting them in a small glass bowl. With a fork, mash the yolks.

Add the salt, pepper, sugar, mustard, cider vinegar, and mayonnaise. Mix well. Spoon the mixture lightly into hollows of the egg whites. Sprinkle the tops with paprika. Place the eggs in a single layer on a platter.

Cover and keep chilled in the refrigerator till serving time.

Serves 6

GILROY STINKING ROSE MUSHROOMS

18

Have plenty of napkins on hand for these drippy, yummy mushrooms.

2 to 3 garlic cloves, finely chopped
½ small chopped sweet onion
3 teaspoons fresh chopped parsley
1 cup finely grated Parmesan cheese
4 tablespoons butter, softened
Freshly ground black pepper to taste
Sea salt to taste
16 large mushrooms, stems removed

In a medium bowl mix all the ingredients except the mushrooms. Fill each mushroom cap with stuffing, mounding it nicely. Place the mushrooms on the barbecue grill over medium direct heat until the mushrooms are lightly browned and cooked soft.

Serves 4 to 8

KARA BETH'S HOT DAMN WINGS

3 to 5 tablespoons Louisiana hot sauce

3 tablespoons vegetable oil

1 tablespoon white vinegar

$\frac{1}{4}$ teaspoon garlic powder

$2\frac{1}{2}$ pounds chicken wings, separated

In a medium mixing bowl, combine the hot sauce, 2 tablespoons of the oil, vinegar, and garlic powder. Pour the sauce into a Ziploc bag, add the chicken wings, and marinate them for at least 2 hours, preferably overnight.

Get a very hot fire going in your barbecue with glowing coals or the gas turned to high. Be sure to brush the grill with the remaining tablespoon of the oil to prevent sticking.

After heating the grill, turn the heat down to medium. Grill the wings for 7 minutes on one side before turning them over for another 7 minutes until nicely browned.

20

Serves 4 to 6

DIXIE WATERMELON SALSA

This salsa is great with steak, roasts, or fish barbecue.

6 cups diced watermelon, seeds removed

1½ cups diced onion

4 to 6 tablespoons jalapeño chili peppers, seeded and finely chopped

3 tablespoons extra virgin olive oil

3 tablespoons red wine vinegar

2 tablespoons fresh lime juice

½ cup finely chopped cilantro

Salt to taste

In a large stainless-steel or glass mixing bowl, combine all the ingredients. Mix well. Chill overnight. Use a half watermelon, which you've hollowed out, as a serving dish, and fill it with the prepared salsa.

21

Serves 4 to 6

MILAN'S COCONUT BABYBACKS

Milan Chuckovich, Vancouver, Washington

Milan is a sweet giant of a man who loves to cook, have friends over for lunch or dinner, and watch his son, Ben, play football. The world could do with many more of him. These ribs are awesome served with garlic mashed potatoes or BBQ sweet potatoes. The soft potatoes complement the meaty texture of the ribs.

5 pounds baby back pork ribs

1 cup canned unsweetened coconut milk

$\frac{1}{2}$ cup chopped fresh basil

$\frac{1}{2}$ cup dark brown sugar

$\frac{1}{3}$ cup chopped shallots

$\frac{1}{4}$ cup teriyaki sauce

3 tablespoons chopped garlic

1 tablespoon peeled and finely chopped fresh ginger

Lemon zest from 2 large lemons, finely chopped

1 teaspoon garlic salt

1 cup toasted coconut flakes

Rinse the ribs. Cut them into single ribs using a "Hollywood cut" (cut the meat close to the bone on the first rib, then cut the meat close to the bone on the third rib, so that you have the second rib bone with more meat on each side).

Combine the coconut milk, basil, brown sugar, shallots, teriyaki sauce, garlic, ginger, lemon zest, and salt into a blender or food processor and pulse-chop until almost smooth.

Place the Hollywood-cut ribs in a 1-gallon, sealable plastic bag and add the marinade. Seal the bag and refrigerate overnight, turning 2 to 3 times.

Heat the coals or briquettes to medium-high. Oil or spray the grill with nonstick spray.

22

Remove the ribs from the marinade and pour the liquid into a medium pan. Boil for at least 10 minutes, but no more than 15 minutes. Cool, add all but 2 tablespoons of the coconut flakes, then use the liquid to baste the ribs. Grill the ribs until browned and tender, basting often. When the ribs are finished, after about 10 minutes, place them in a large, covered baking dish or on a large piece of heavy-duty aluminum foil, brush heavily with the marinade, sprinkle with the remaining coconut flakes, seal the foil, and set away from the heat until ready to serve.

Serves 4

007 MARTINI OYSTERS

These oysters are perfect when served with lots of ice-cold vodka in chilled shot glasses.

1 cup vodka
2 tablespoons finely chopped green olives
1 tablespoon finely chopped shallots
Small dash of vermouth (optional)
12 large oysters on the half shell
Freshly ground black pepper to taste

Put the vodka, olives, and shallots in an 8-ounce plastic container. Add the vermouth, if desired. Shake well, do not stir, and put the container in the freezer for at least a day.

Build a hot fire in the grill using charcoal, wood, or briquettes. Shuck the oysters and put each half shell containing the oyster on the grill, saving as much of the natural juices as you can.

Drizzle the martini mixture over each oyster, and cook just until the edges curl. Liberally grind pepper over each oyster.

Remove from the grill and serve.

Serves 4 to 6

23

SCOTCH-SMOKED TROUT OR SALMON

Grant and June Browne, Kimberly, British Columbia, Canada

Serve this fish with rye or pumpernickel bread and unsalted butter. Garnish with small gherkins or cornichons.

WET BRINE

3 cups water

1 cup dry white wine

$\frac{1}{2}$ cup light brown sugar

20 juniper berries, ground

$\frac{1}{2}$ cup pickling spices

4 teaspoons coarse salt

3 tablespoons cracked black pepper

Zest of 2 lemons, finely chopped

Whole fish, butterflied, or fillet of fish (salmon, trout, shark, or halibut)

Heat the water and wine in a medium pan and bring to a boil over high heat, add the brown sugar, and quickly reduce the heat to medium-low and stir until the sugar dissolves. Add the berries, pickling spices, salt, pepper, and zest. Cover, reduce the heat to simmer, and cook for 1 hour. Remove the mixture from the heat, strain the brine through a cheesecloth, discard the spices, and cool the brine in the refrigerator.

Lay the fillet or whole butterflied fish in a large glass or ceramic dish

24

and cover with cold brine. Cover the dish with plastic wrap or aluminum foil, and refrigerate overnight. If you don't have that much time, follow these guidelines for *minimum* times to brine fish.

COOKING TIMES

Fish thickness	Fat fish	Lean fish
$\frac{3}{4}$"	$2\frac{1}{2}$ hrs	$1\frac{1}{2}$ hrs
1"	$3\frac{1}{2}$ hrs	$2\frac{1}{2}$ hrs
$1\frac{1}{4}$"	$4\frac{3}{4}$ hrs	$3\frac{1}{4}$ hrs
$1\frac{1}{2}$"	6 hrs	4 hrs
$1\frac{3}{4}$"	$7\frac{1}{4}$ hrs	$4\frac{3}{4}$ hrs
2"	$9\frac{1}{2}$ hrs	$6\frac{1}{2}$ hrs
$2\frac{1}{2}$"	12 hrs	8 hrs
3"	$14\frac{1}{4}$ hrs	$9\frac{1}{2}$ hrs

These times are just a guide; each variety of fish reacts somewhat differently. When done, the flesh will be firm enough for slicing and feel like the lean part of a slab of bacon when pressed with a finger.

Prepare the barbecue for smoking at 200° to 220°F, placing a medium pan filled with 1 inch or so of water under the grill where the fish will rest. Using the indirect cooking method (see page 6), cook the fish on the cool side of the grill.

Remove the fish from the brine, pat it dry, and place it, skin side down, on the grill. Discard the brine. Cover and smoke the fish over aromatic wood smoke for 2 to $2\frac{1}{2}$ hours until its internal temperature is 140° to 145°F. (For tips on scented wood grilling, see page 254).

Can be served warm or cold, sliced very thinly.

MIKEY'S MELBOURNE CRAB DAMPER

Michael Coyne, Melbourne, Australia

Michael is a fine chap who often says, "Some bread and a piece of cheese would do fine" when asked what he wants for a meal, but who is a Tasmanian devil in the kitchen whipping up Down Under culinary wonders.

26

3 cups buttermilk

1 cup heavy cream

$\frac{1}{2}$ teaspoon paprika

1 teaspoon garlic salt

$\frac{1}{4}$ teaspoon pepper

1 cup yellow cornmeal

$\frac{1}{4}$ cup melted butter

2 cups crabmeat (Dungeness or other
    local favorite), cooked

4 eggs, beaten

1 small can green chili peppers, mild or hot

1 cup cubed Emmenthaler cheese

Zesty Lemon Butter (see recipe below)

Combine the buttermilk, cream, paprika, garlic salt, and pepper in a medium saucepan. Heat over medium heat until just warm and well mixed, then add the cornmeal, stirring constantly until smooth and heated through. Reduce the heat to low. Add the butter, crabmeat, eggs, green chilis, and cheese, and stir for 3 minutes. Pour the batter into a large, greased cast-iron pot. As the bread will rise, make sure there are 2 inches of pot above the batter.

Place the pot in a smoker, or a kettle-type barbecue, on the opposite side of the grill from the coals, gas burners, or briquettes, and cook for 40 to 50 minutes at about 250°F, or until the surface is golden brown and a toothpick inserted into the middle comes out clean. Cool slightly, take out of the cast-iron pot, and cut into 8 pieces. Serve with lemon butter.

Serves 8

ZESTY LEMON BUTTER

Juice of 1 lemon
1 tablespoon finely chopped lemon zest
1 teaspoon finely chopped fresh parsley
Pinch of salt
2 sticks softened butter
Sprinkle of paprika

27

Mix the lemon juice, zest, parsley, and salt into the softened butter. Mold into a small round dish, sprinkle with paprika, and chill.

Kansas City Barbecue Society cofounder Carolyn Wells (far right) yuks it up at the California BBQ championships.

SMOKY WILD MUSHROOM TART

2 ounces each dried porcini, cèpe, oyster
    mushrooms, shiitakes, and chanterelles

1 medium red onion

2 tablespoons butter

$\frac{1}{4}$ cup extra virgin olive oil

2 tablespoons dried parsley

1 tablespoon dried savory

1 tablespoon dried sage

$\frac{1}{2}$ cup fresh wild mushrooms (from the market)

1 portobello mushroom, cut in $\frac{1}{4}$-inch strips
    ($\frac{1}{2}$ cup)

3 tablespoons tomato paste

1 cup beef (or chicken) stock

4 eggs

$\frac{3}{4}$ cup freshly grated Parmesan cheese

2 tablespoons Jack Daniel's whiskey

Salt and lemon pepper to taste

1 precooked 10-inch tart pastry shell in
    aluminum foil

30

Reconstitute the dried mushrooms in warm water for 20 minutes and set them aside.

Chop the onion and sauté in the butter and olive oil until translucent, then add the dried herbs and cook for an additional 2 minutes. Add the fresh mushrooms, the reconstituted dried mushrooms, tomato paste, and stock, and simmer for a few minutes until the mixture thickens, then remove from the heat and let the mixture cool completely.

Whip the eggs in a bowl and add to a medium bowl along with $\frac{1}{2}$ cup of the cheese. Add the Jack Daniel's and season with salt and pepper. Stir until well mixed.

Pour the filling into the pastry shell and bake in a 350° to 375°F barbecue grill or smoker for about 25 minutes over indirect heat using hickory, cherry, or alderwood chips for added flavor. The top of the tart will be nicely browned and moderately firm to the touch. A knife or toothpick inserted into the filling should come out clean.

Remove the tart from the smoker and let it firm up, covered, for about 10 minutes. Sprinkle the tart with the remaining $\frac{1}{2}$ cup cheese, slice, and serve warm.

Serves 6 to 8

31

TENNY LAMAS, FRICKLES, AND ROCKIES

30th Annual World's Championship Bar-B-Que Contest

HOUSTON, TEXAS

It's probably the biggest dang barbecue event in America, or in the world for that matter. A competition that spans 45 acres, involves more than 350 teams (some containing as many as 50 members), consumes more than 100,000 pounds of BBQ'd meat, and last year attracted more than 170,000 people during its three-day life span.

They call it the World's Championship Bar-B-Que Contest, even though the teams are all from the U.S., and in fact are almost 100 percent from the host state itself. Other contests with "International" or "World" in their names actually invite participants from foreign countries. Here the world includes . . . Texas.

It's a wonderful event nonetheless, and despite its humble beginnings three decades ago, it is now one of the biggest events in a big-oriented state. Started as a friendly competition in the driveway beside the Astrodome, with a gathering of volunteers, pickup trucks, some coolers, and a bunch of backyard barbecue grills, the event has grown into the largest charitable barbecue event in the world, and a vital component of the Houston Stock Show and Rodeo itself. Last year the proceeds from the barbecue and rodeo, run by an all-volunteer army of more than 13,000, raised just a tad under $10 million for local scholarships, FFA and 4-H groups, graduate assistantships, college and university endowments, research programs, and the Rodeo Institute for Teacher Excellence.

And, typical of anything Texan, they serve BIG amounts of grub there, too. Hired cooks dish up thousands of pounds of beef brisket, pork ribs, and chicken. That's not to mention the fried pickles, sausages, potato salad, coleslaw, burgers, hams, game hens, beefsteaks, hot dogs, guacamole, beans, garlic bread, nachos, tortillas, and other comestibles served to legions of ten gallon–hatted guests in the swarming corporate tents. To wash it all down, the cowboys 'n' cowgals quaff an Olympic swimming pool–sized amount of beer and "sodey pop" (over 24,000 cases in all), chilled by 300,000 pounds of ice—all in three days!

Unlike other U.S. Que competitions, which involve either amateur cooks or which have a separate category for the sport's "pros," the Houston BBQ event has a unique format that has corporate teams hiring professional cooks, chefs, and pitmasters to represent and cook up a storm for their team. The cooks compete in three categories: beef brisket (after all, this is Texas, where brisket *is* barbecue), chicken, and pork ribs, and each team must turn in 10 pounds of meat to the judges in one of those three categories. Judging is done on appearance, aroma, tenderness, and (most important) taste.

But unlike other contests, there is zero prize money. Remember, all proceeds go to scholarships and education funds. The winner receives merely a whole buncha braggin' rights. Again this is Texas, certainly the inventor and copyright holder of braggin' rights.

Other "competitions" include Most Unique Pit, Most Colorful Team, Best Team Skit, Best Recycling Team, Cleanest Team Area, and last but not least: the Best Butt Contest. No, not the cooked pork shoulder kind of butt. This fiercely battled match is for lithe, and some not-so-lithe, ladies who appear to delight in showing off their, well . . . assets, wearing the delightful and very form-fitting regional apparel— Rockies jeans. Which, the manufacturer shyly admits, "have been designed in a style that flatters your hip line and buttocks." Yup, it does.

This, by the way, is the only competition at the barbecue championships that

has more eager "volunteer judges," both professional and amateur, in attendance than all the BBQ categories and rodeo competitions put together.

On my visit, I saw another fashion statement traipsing across the sauce-dribbled parking lot, which must have been originated by the likes of Garth Brooks, George Strait, and Alan Jackson: the predominance of black hats. My heavens, I thought I was at a convention of Hollywood cowboy bad guys, with nary a good guy white hat to be seen. I reckon the ten-gallon *noir* look is IN these days! Roy and Gene and Hopalong are all probably shaking their heads in wonder.

And while we're speaking of fashion, let me mention the "Tenny Lamas" boot — er shoe, er high-top sneakers — tons of folks have a hankerin' fer down here. For these cowpokes and cowpokettes there is now a canvas-and-rubber substitute so you can achieve that "wrangler look" without putting your tootsies in them hotter 'n'-the-El-Paso-sun-in-July leather boots.

When not noting the western fashion scene, I spent most of my time, other than a few very brief moments at that Best Butt competition, with cook/caterer Carl Triola and his delightful family in the Damnifino team tent. Its twenty-three members each paid $500 to help defray the costs of setting up the tent, buying hundreds of pounds of meat, taters and beans, and barrels of adult liquid refreshments for what only seemed like half the population of Houston.

Every evening the "hospitality" flowed, as long as you had the right color bracelet or scarf to let you into the private BBQ parties, that is, and hundreds of pounds of barbecued, fried, broiled, baked, and sautéed chow were downed by the truckloads of corporate guests, friends of the team, scattered members of the press, and more than a few stunning Texas damsels (many wearing those durn Rockies) who somehow got past the guards flashing nothing but smiles.

Damnifino's membership list reads like a country club roster. It includes real estate brokers, a trucking company owner, electrical contractors, oil field and chemical executives, mortgage brokers, real estate developers, home builders, venture capitalists, business owners, a neurosurgeon, an oncologist, and (most appropriate for the cholesterol orgy going on in the background) a cardiologist. Luck was with us and no one required his services that night. Pass another fried rib with ranch dressing, please.

Not a poor man's sport this. But remember all that money goes to a good purpose. So good in fact that since its inception in 1957 the rodeo, and the barbecue competition, which began in 1973, have poured more than *$85 million* toward education. Since ya gotta eat anyway . . .

Other than expanding our waistline by several magnitudes we learned many things during our three days in Houston. We learned about "frickles" (fried pickles), we were shown how to do "pitchfork" steaks, we discerned the difference between the "slide" and the "two-step," we watched how to cook up "real" Texas beans, and we finally figured out why brisket takes so danged long to cook right. At the same time we decided that Texas hospitality is as friendly and warm as we've ever experienced anywhere. We really felt deep in the heart of Texas.

And, oh yes, we discovered where we can order up a pair o' them Rockies jeans for the missus back home.

2 BEEF

BIG AL'S SMOKED CHILI

Al Meek, Runnells, Iowa

Serve warm with grilled bread that has been rubbed with garlic and then buttered.

$\frac{1}{2}$ pound ground beef

2 cups brown sugar

$\frac{1}{4}$ cup Worcestershire sauce

$\frac{1}{8}$ cup yellow mustard

1 tablespoon your favorite dry rub

$\frac{1}{2}$ medium onion, chopped

Two 28-ounce cans Bush's baked beans

Cook the ground beef in a cast-iron frying pan over medium-high heat for approximately 15 minutes, or until well browned. Add the brown sugar, Worcestershire sauce, mustard, dry rub, and onion, and stir well. Add the beans and stir. Cook, uncovered, in a 250° to 275°F smoker for approximately 2 hours, over indirect heat, stirring every 30 minutes, or until you reach the desired consistency.

39

Serves 4 to 6

Check out this hand-carved Estonian wood stump smoker!

CHEESE-Y BBQED ROAST BEEF

Don Havranek, Smokin in Montana Team

INJECTION

1 cup water

3 beef bouillon cubes

1-inch slice Velveeta cheese
   (about 2 ounces)

$\frac{1}{4}$ cup butter

$4\frac{1}{2}$ pounds beef roast

RUB

$\frac{1}{2}$ teaspoon granulated garlic

1 teaspoon cayenne pepper

2 teaspoons seasoned salt

Cracked black pepper

40

On low heat in a medium saucepan, dissolve all the injection ingredients. While still hot, place a large-bore needle into the mixture and, by raising the plunger, suck it into the syringe (you need a large-bore needle because of the thick melted cheese). Inject the mixture thoroughly into the meat. Rub the roast with the garlic, cayenne, seasoned salt, and black pepper. Cover with plastic wrap and refrigerate for 12 hours or overnight.

Get a good hot fire going on the grill with mesquite briquettes or chunks that have been placed on one side of the grill only (see page 6 on indirect grilling). Sear the roast for 5 to 10 minutes on both sides over the hot side of the grill, over the mesquite briquettes. Move the meat to the cool side of the grill to grill indirectly (ideally with a temperature of approximately 300° to 350°F), which may take up to an hour.

Take the meat off the grill when the internal temperature is 145° to 150°F. Cover with aluminum foil and allow to set for 15 minutes before carving.

Serves 6 to 8

Two emergency-room doctors, crossing their marinade injectors, make up the Big Bee Que team, Columbus, Georgia.

DAN AND RON'S TRI-TIP ROAST

Dan Brodsky and Ron Jessen,
Scotts Valley, California

Serve with garlic mashed potatoes or on buttered and grilled hoagie or Kaiser rolls.

One 4- to 5-pound tri-tip beef roast
3 tablespoons minced garlic
1 large onion, chopped
$\frac{1}{4}$ cup melted clarified butter
$\frac{1}{4}$ cup olive oil
$\frac{1}{4}$ cup A-1 steak sauce
1 teaspoon Louisiana hot sauce
1 cup teriyaki sauce
1 cup Chianti
Several long rosemary branches, tied at
    one end to form a basting brush

Put the roast into a 1-gallon Ziploc bag, add the rest of the ingredients, except the rosemary branches, and marinate overnight in the refrigerator.

Remove the meat from the marinade and set aside. Pour the reserved marinade into a small saucepan and bring it to a boil for at least 10 minutes so it will be safe to use as a marinade. Let it cool. Use the rosemary brush to baste the meat once every half hour during the $1\frac{1}{2}$ hour cooking time. You can leave the brush standing in the marinade between basting sessions.

Using the indirect method for a barbecue or gas grill, prepare a medium-hot fire (450° to 500°F). Place the meat over direct heat for 5 minutes a side, then transfer it to the side of barbecue that is unheated. Cook for 1 to $1\frac{1}{2}$ hours until the meat is evenly browned and has an internal temperature of 135° to 140°F.

Seal the meat in aluminum foil for 15 minutes, and the meat's internal temperature should reach 145°F (medium rare) in that time.

Slice thinly.

Serves 8 to 10

DR PEPPER BEEF BRISKET

Donald R. Wallace, San Antonio, Texas

2 cans Dr Pepper
2 beef bouillon cubes, dissolved in 4 ounces water
4 garlic cloves, minced
1 tablespoon Worcestershire sauce
2 tablespoons lime or lemon juice
12 ounces barbecue sauce, your favorite
McCormick Montreal steak seasoning
Freshly ground black pepper
One 10- to 12-pound brisket

Combine all the ingredients in a plastic bag. Marinate the brisket for 2 days. Early in the morning of the day you are going to cook it, remove the brisket from the marinade and let it sit at room temperature while you get the fire ready. Pour the marinade into a small saucepan and boil for at least 10 minutes, cool, and put in a sealable bottle.

Place the brisket in a smoker, or on indirect heat in a barbecue grill, fat side up, and cook for 12 to 14 hours at 225° to 250°F. I usually start about 7:00 or 8:00 in the morning and take the meat off the smoker at about 10:00 or 11:00 that night. Baste during cooking with the marinade (remember, it has to be boiled first). After 12 to 14 hours of cooking, the brisket should be almost all black and look like you've burned it—you haven't.

Remove the brisket from the smoker, baste liberally with marinade,

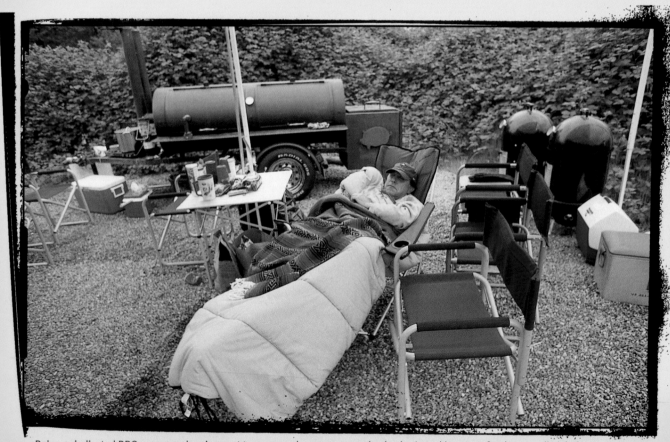

Being a dedicated BBQer means sleeping next to your smoker so you can check what's cooking every few hours—all night long.

and wrap in heavy-duty aluminum foil. Wrap it a second time. Place the brisket in the foil in the smoker or in the barbecue, and let it cook overnight at 150° to 160°F. About 1:00 or 2:00 the next afternoon, you got the best-tasting, juiciest, and most tender brisket you have ever had. The internal temperature should be around 160° to 170°F.

Note: If all else fails and it rains, or you can't use a smoker, you can put the roast (uncovered) in a Pyrex pan or roasting pan in your kitchen oven, set the temperature to 220°F, and cook for 10 hours. Add a pinch of liquid smoke or Oregon Spice Company's Natural Mesquite Smoke Powder (oregonspice.com) to your BBQ sauce and you'll be amazed at the results.

Serves 10 to 12

GRILLED HUNTSMAN BEEF SANDWICHES

Serve with shoestring potatoes or barbecued beans.

1 cup crumbled Huntsman cheese

2 tablespoons mayonnaise

1 teaspoon prepared horseradish

Sea salt to taste

Cracked black pepper to taste

8 slices sourdough bread

$1\frac{1}{2}$ pounds sliced rare roast beef

1 sweet Walla Walla onion, thinly sliced

1 large Gala apple, thinly sliced

4 tablespoons butter, melted

Mix the cheese, mayonnaise, and horseradish in a small glass bowl until relatively smooth (there will still be lumps of cheese in the mixture). Add salt and pepper.

45

Spread the mixture thickly on each slice of bread. Top each of 4 bread slices with one-quarter of the beef, then with the onion and apple. Top with the remaining slices of bread, the cheese-mayonnaise-horseradish side down.

Brush the melted butter on top of the bread and turn that side down on the grill, cook over medium coals (400° to 500°F) until golden, about 2 minutes. Butter the top slice of bread, then turn it over and grill for about another 2 minutes.

Serves 4

GRILLED SHALLOT-COGNAC STEAKS

These are stuffed with shallots, green onions, and shiitake mushrooms. Serve with dirty rice (see page 182) and barbecued vegetables.

1 tablespoon extra virgin olive oil

$\frac{1}{2}$ cup very finely chopped shallots

$\frac{1}{2}$ cup chopped shiitake mushrooms

$\frac{1}{2}$ cup thinly sliced green onions

$\frac{1}{4}$ teaspoon salt

$\frac{1}{4}$ teaspoon pepper

$\frac{1}{8}$ cup cognac

2 boneless beef top-loin steaks,
    cut 2 inches thick, about 1 pound each

Wooden toothpicks, soaked for
    20 minutes in hot water

In a small nonstick skillet, heat the olive oil over medium heat until hot. Add the shallots and mushrooms, and cook 4 to 5 minutes, or until tender. Then add the green onions and continue cooking and stirring 4 to 5 min-

46

utes, or until the onions are tender. Remove from the heat. Add the salt, pepper, and cognac, and cool completely.

Meanwhile, with a sharp knife, make a pocket in each steak by cutting horizontally along one long side to within $\frac{1}{2}$ inch of each of the other three sides. Spread half of the shallot-onion-mushroom mixture inside each pocket. Secure the pockets with 2 to 3 toothpicks.

Place the steaks on the grill over the highest gas setting or white ash–covered coals at 600° to 700°F. Grill, covered with the barbecue lid. Turn the steaks after 6 to 8 minutes (twice per side), cooking them according to the guidelines below for 2-inch steaks. At each turning, rotate the steaks 45 degrees to vary the grill marks. Steaks are cooked to medium rare at a 145°F internal temperature, medium at 160°F. Well done (if you really must ruin a good steak) is "ready" at 170°F.

Remove the toothpicks. Carve the steaks crosswise into $\frac{1}{2}$-inch-thick slices.

STEAK GRILLING GUIDELINES

THICKNESS	RARE	MEDIUM	WELL	HEAT
1''	8–10 min	12–14 min	16–20 min	High
1½''	10–14 min	16–20 min	22–26 min	High
2''	12–16 min	18–22 min	24–28 min	High

These times are total cooking times. Divide in half for each side. Times are approximate and will vary depending on the type of grill, fuel, weather conditions, etc.

Serves 6

HONEY-MUSTARD GRILLED RIB-EYE STEAKS

48

1 cup yellow mustard

2 tablespoons chopped fresh parsley

2 tablespoons crushed rosemary leaves

2 tablespoons crushed thyme

4 tablespoons honey

¼ cup cider vinegar

1 tablespoon Worcestershire sauce

1 cup water

½ teaspoon Louisiana hot sauce

¼ teaspoon coarse black pepper

Four 1-inch-thick rib-eye steaks

RB's BBQ Steak Sauce (see recipe below)

4 pats butter

Mix the first 10 ingredients well in a large bowl, reserve half of the resulting liquid and put in a small bowl, pour the remainder of the liquid over the rib-eye steaks in a 10 × 12-inch, flat Pyrex dish and marinate for 30 minutes, turning the steaks over several times. Poke the steaks several times with a fork so the marinade gets into the center of the meat.

Put the reserved marinade in a small saucepan and boil for 10 minutes, then you can safely use it to brush on the steaks.

Turn the steaks with tongs, *not* a fork, and cook on a hot grill (500° to 600°F or higher if using mesquite) or very hot coals for 5 to 6 minutes a side for medium rare. Brush generously with the reserved, boiled marinade once or twice per side.

Drizzle steak sauce (see recipe below) on each plate. Place a small pat of butter on top of each steak and serve.

Serves 4

RB'S BBQ STEAK SAUCE

1 cup of your favorite Cattlemen's barbecue sauce

3 tablespoons maple syrup

1 teaspoon dried summer savory

$\frac{1}{2}$ teaspoons cayenne pepper

1 tablespoon olive oil

1 tablespoon lime juice

Mix all the ingredients in a large bowl, put in a plastic squeeze bottle, and drizzle over the plates before you put the steaks on them. Or serve warm in a gravy boat or sauce dish along with the steaks.

Makes $\frac{1}{4}$ cup

INEBRIATED TOP ROUND

MARINADE

$\frac{1}{2}$ cup red wine

1 cup Jack Daniel's Tennessee sippin' whiskey

$\frac{1}{4}$ cup beer

$\frac{1}{4}$ cup balsamic vinegar

2 tablespoons finely chopped onion

2 teaspoons finely chopped garlic

1 teaspoon dried tarragon

1 teaspoon fresh or dried rosemary leaves

$\frac{1}{2}$ teaspoon pepper

$\frac{1}{2}$ cup brown sugar

$1\frac{1}{2}$ to 2 pounds top round beefsteak

2 teaspoons sea salt

Dash of steak sauce

Mix the first 10 ingredients in a large ceramic bowl. Generously salt the meat with the sea salt and put it in a Ziploc bag. Pour the marinade into the bag and shake it to coat the meat well. Place the sealed bag in a large dish (in case the plastic leaks) and refrigerate for 24 hours, turning the bag over 2 to 3 times.

Remove the steak from the refrigerator and let it come to room temperature. Pour the reserved marinade into a medium saucepan and boil for at least 10 minutes. Add the steak sauce. Cool the marinade and put it in a sealed jar.

When you're ready to cook the meat, preheat the barbecue to medium-high heat.

50

When the coals reach 400° to 500°F, place the meat on an oiled grill 4 inches from medium-hot coals and cook for 12 to 16 minutes total, 6 to 8 minutes per side or to desired doneness. Baste occasionally with the marinade.

Cut the steak across the grain into thin slices and serve on a very hot platter.

Serves 4

MARINATED DINOSAUR RIBS

2 to 3 racks of beef ribs
2 cups orange juice
½ cup extra virgin olive oil
½ cup balsamic vinegar
½ cup Worcestershire sauce
1 tablespoon garlic salt
1 tablespoon dry mustard
1 teaspoon paprika
1 teaspoon chili powder
1 teaspoon Louisiana hot sauce

Preheat the grill to medium high (450° to 550°F), using the indirect method (see page 6). You will cook the meat on the side of the grill that is away from the heat.

For more tender ribs peel off the membrane on the backside of the rack, using a towel or paper towel to grip the membrane.

Mix together all the remaining ingredients, except the ribs, in a large bowl. Place the ribs in a dish or Ziploc bag, pour in the marinade, and marinate in the refrigerator for 4 to 6 hours. Reserving the marinade, drain the ribs and set them aside until they reach room temperature. Put the marinade in a medium saucepan and boil it for at least 10 minutes. Remove the marinade from the heat, cool, and reserve.

Once the grill has reached 450° to 550°F, cook the ribs over indirect heat (cool side) for 1 hour, basting very frequently with the marinade. Remove the ribs from the grill and place the ribs on heavy-duty aluminum foil, baste both sides lavishly, seal the foil, and set aside for 10 to 15 minutes to cool and become infused with the marinade.

Open the foil packages at the table and dig in.

Serves 6 to 10

RODNEY'S TEQUILA PORTERHOUSE

Rodney Patten, somewhere over Montana, was a true friend who loved good barbecue, to laugh, and everyone he met.

$\frac{1}{4}$ cup soy sauce

$\frac{1}{2}$ cup extra virgin olive oil

4 ounces good-quality tequila

2 pounds choice porterhouse steak, aged

1 crushed garlic clove

2 tablespoons lime juice

2 tablespoons pineapple juice

$\frac{1}{4}$ cup melted butter

Dash of balsamic vinegar

2 teaspoons lemon pepper

2 teaspoons McCormick Montreal
spicy steak seasoning

Mix the soy sauce, olive oil, and 2 ounces of the tequila together in a small container and shake until well mixed. Put the steak into a Ziploc bag, pour in the marinade, and marinate at room temperature for 1 hour. Drain the steak, discarding the marinade.

Mix the remaining ingredients, except for the tequila, in a small bowl. Apply to both sides of the meat, rubbing in well with your hands.

Place the steak on the grill over a hot mesquite fire (600° to 700°F), and cook until you reach the desired state, approximately 6 to 8 minutes per side for medium rare. Place the meat on a platter and drizzle the extra tequila over both sides of the steak just before serving.

Do not pour liquor over the meat while it is over or near an open flame unless you want to be an ignited part of the barbecue yourself!!

Serves 4 to 6

SPATS' GRILLED MEATBALLS

To my best buddy, who always wears a tux and spats.

MEATBALLS

$\frac{3}{4}$ pound ground chuck
$\frac{3}{4}$ pound ground turkey
$1\frac{1}{2}$ cups fine fresh bread crumbs
1 large egg
$\frac{1}{4}$ cup finely chopped shallots
1 teaspoon granulated garlic
$\frac{1}{2}$ teaspoon ground nutmeg
$\frac{1}{4}$ teaspoon cinnamon
1 tablespoon dried basil
$\frac{1}{2}$ teaspoon salt
Lemon pepper to taste

SAUCE

$\frac{1}{3}$ cup honey Dijon mustard
$\frac{1}{3}$ cup packed brown sugar
3 tablespoons balsamic vinegar
2 tablespoons extra virgin olive oil
2 tablespoons finely chopped Italian parsley

Preheat the grill to medium (400° to 500°F). Soak 12 bamboo skewers in warm water for 30 minutes.

In a large bowl, with your hands blend together all the meatball ingredients until well combined. Roll the mixture into $1\frac{1}{4}$-inch balls and arrange on a platter, cover, and chill for at least 30 minutes.

In a bowl whisk all the sauce ingredients together until the sugar is dissolved. Cover and chill for 30 minutes.

55

Thread 4 to 6 meatballs onto each skewer. Prepare the grill by heating briquettes or chunks of charcoal so they are glowing (covered with a slight white-ash covering). If using gas, prepare a very hot fire.

Grill the kebabs on an oiled rack set 5 to 6 inches over the briquettes, charcoal chunks, or gas, turning them frequently. Brush the meatballs with sauce frequently, turning often until cooked through, or 5 to 10 minutes.

Serves 6 to 8

TANG-Y GRILL-ROAST PRIME RIB

One 12- to 15-pound prime rib, bone in, cap off

RUB

1 cup kosher salt

1 cup coarse cracked black pepper

$\frac{1}{2}$ cup Tang (orange breakfast drink)

$\frac{1}{4}$ cup granulated garlic

5 whole garlic cloves, sliced thinly

56

In a small bowl combine salt, pepper, Tang, and granulated garlic, then rub into the meat.

With a sharp knife cut slits in the meat and insert slices of garlic in each slit.

In a large kettle grill, mound charcoal well over to one side, place an aluminum 9 × 12-inch pan, filled with 1 to 2 inches of water, on the other side of the coal bed. Place the grill above the coals. When the coals are glowing, at about 350° to 400°F, place the prime rib on the grill on the side opposite the coals, being careful that no part of the rib is directly over the coals. Put the lid on the kettle with the vents one-quarter open. Cook for approximately 2 hours, adding a handful of fresh charcoal every

30 minutes or so. If using a gas grill, turn the gas jets on medium high on the side away from the meat.

At the 2-hour point, check the rib with a meat thermometer to determine doneness; remove from the fire at 130°F for rare, 140°F for medium rare, 160°F for medium, and so on, adding 4°F for each degree of doneness.

Remove from the heat, seal in aluminum foil, and allow to rest for 30 minutes before slicing.

Serves 8 to 10

Who stole the damn food?

★ BBQ ON THE ★ SAMMISH SLOUGH

Pacific Northwest Barbecue Association Regional Championship

RED HOOK ALE BREWERY, WOODINVILLE, WASHINGTON

In one of the most idyllic settings we visited on our entire barbecue pilgrimage across the fruited plains of the U.S., we delighted in the quiet, calm, and peaceful setting of the Pacific Northwest's biggest barbecue event in the tiny town of Woodinville, about thirty minutes north of Seattle.

Held in the parklike setting of the Red Hook Ale Brewery, in a rural area scattered with upscale wineries and rolling vineyards, sits the venue for what proved to be a delightfully calm, cool, and collected event. Forget the madness of Houston, the frenzy of Memphis, or the bustle of Kansas City's American Royal. The PNWBA Championships were almost lethargic in tone, but delightfully slow, not boring.

Until the meat went on the barbecues, that is. Then serious cooks and serious-er judges took over, and the reverence put on properly cooked meat, poultry, and fish matched the largest contests in the land. Barbecuing may be

fun, but it's also a serious business, even among the neighborly folks of the Pacific Northwest.

Under Kansas City Barbecue Society contest rules (KCBS sanctions more than five hundred contests across the country), the teams compete in brisket, chicken, pork ribs, pork shoulder and, yes, we are close to the Pacific, salmon. And not just any salmon, mind you. Here they cook up the premier variety of this species. The Mercedes-Benz, Cartier, or Gucci of salmon: Copper River sockeye from the Gulf of Alaska.

If you've ever shopped at a market for this famed variety of fish, you've missed a grate, I mean GREAT, culinary barbecue treat. The cold rushing waters of the Copper River produce some of the richest, most naturally succulent salmon in the world. Wild Copper River Chinook (king), sockeye (red), and coho (silver) salmon—with their rich color, firm texture, and wonderful flavor—are renowned throughout the world. And lucky are the folks who live in the Pacific Northwest, where the spring brings these luscious fish to our markets.

The Copper River terminates in the gulf and is one of the most pristine river systems in the world. Because of its three-hundred-mile length and the challenges of its hundreds of rapids, the salmon that originate here are noted for their firm, bright red flesh, nutty flavor, and the extra oils and fat that they carry to fuel them on their migration to their spawning grounds. The king and red salmon, arriving in early May, are the first of the season to return to the rivers and streams of Alaska. Fortunately for those of us who appreciate their rich flavor and firm texture, the fats and Omega-3 oils are the kinds that your cardiologist would recommend. Fatty fish, yes, but a good fat that!

Red salmon are the second most abundant species of salmon in Alaska. Red salmon spend one to four years in the Pacific Ocean and reach sizes of four to seven pounds. Red salmon range far and wide in the nutrient-rich waters of the North Pacific, feeding on natural plankton and fishes before returning to fresh water to spawn. King salmon may migrate to the marine environment the spring after they hatch, or they can spend up to two years in the riparian environment prior to migrating out to sea. King salmon spend five years or more in the ocean, reaching sizes of up to sixty pounds before returning to spawn.

The Car Dogs Barbecue Team, which consists of the dynamic duo of Jack Rogers and Jim Minion, took us under their wing, or rather fin, and acted not only as our hosts, explaining the inner workings of this particular contest, but fed us until we near burst, provided liquid refreshment on an unusually tepid Pacific Northwest day, and even shared some of their award-winning recipes with us.

Jack demonstrated how to remove the pin bones from a fillet (use strong tweezers or needle-nose pliers), and Jim shared their double-rub method of cooking salmon, which won a recent Canadian championship in a British Columbia barbecue competition, and which placed second at the Red Hook event. We also share it with readers in the recipe section of this chapter.

We watched as fillets were rubbed, marinated, salted, peppered, fruited, smoked, grilled, sauced, drizzled with butter or lemon or bourbon, and gobbled up in seconds once the judges had their portion delivered to their lofty perch in a room atop the brewery.

Simply put, what we tasted was the best salmon any of us had ever wrapped our teeth around. Consider the quality of the fish itself, its freshness; twenty-four hours out of the Gulf of Alaska, or as Jack put it, "one day from brine to broiler." Put the fillets in the hands of some of America's best barbecue cooks (who've won categories in the major national BBQ contests: Jack Daniel's, Memphis in May, and the American Royal), and you have the best of the best cooking the best.

Not to demean the pork butts, ribs, beef briskets, or chicken samples we were offered and hungrily gobbled. The Deep South and America's BBQ heartland aside, the quality of barbecue, especially competitive barbecue, has almost leveled off. That means that nowadays the incredible taste of a good rib, a slice of beer-can chicken, or hunk of brisket is as good north of Seattle as it is south of the Mason-Dixon line.

We saw North Carolina vinegar sauce dribbled on pork butt, Georgia mustard sauce glazing baby back ribs, Pacific Rim–style teriyaki-hoisin marinades used on Texas brisket, and hot curry rubs inspired by tandoori barbecue used on salmon fillets that were one day earlier swimming in the Gulf of Alaska.

Thanks to fervent barbecuers like the folks smoking on the banks of the Sammish Slough, BBQ has spread across the country like wildfire, and finally people are trying other regional rubs, sauces, meats, and cooking styles, and discarding their old provincial "we don't do it that way here" disdain of Que practiced in other places.

First it was the South, then it moved west, then to the shores of the Atlantic, and to the middle of America, and now good, no, GREAT barbecue is being done from coast to coast. America is pretty much BBQ'd up.

Now it's time to Que the world!

63

3
FISH AND SHELLFISH

AUNT LILLY'S SIZZLING LOBSTER

Richard Westhaver, Norwell, Massachusetts

Richard's aunt Lilly was from a fourth generation of Gloucester fishermen and could grill up some great lobsters. She swears this is the exact recipe she uses. I'm not sure about that, but it's close enough for me and an excellent recipe either way.

2 shallots, minced

4 garlic cloves, mashed

1 pound salted butter

$\frac{1}{4}$ cup chopped fresh parsley

$\frac{2}{3}$ cup fresh lemon juice

Juice of $\frac{1}{2}$ medium orange

2 tablespoons fresh tarragon

Salt and pepper to taste

Four 2-pound live Maine lobsters

Fresh lemon wedges

Sauté the shallots and garlic in a medium saucepan for 5 minutes, or until soft. Add the rest of the ingredients, except the lobster and the lemon wedges, and heat them until the butter is melted. Lower the heat to the lowest setting and keep the butter warm, stirring occasionally. Line the grill with aluminum foil, and prepare a medium-hot fire (450° to 500°F).

Split each lobster by placing it on its back, severing the spinal cord by inserting a sharp knife between the tail and body, then splitting the lobster in half lengthwise. Remove the stomach and intestinal vein. Paint the lobster with the melted butter mixture and place it on the grill flesh side down, cooking until there is a light char on the meat. Turn, baste with butter, and grill until the meat is firm.

Remove the claws from the lobster and leave them on the grill for 5 to 6 minutes more. Remove the rest of the lobster from the grill, paint it with melted butter, and wrap it in foil. Remove the claws from the grill, unwrap the lobster, and serve it with the melted butter and lemon wedges.

Serves 4

66

CAR DOGS'
AWARD-WINNING SALMON

Jim Minion and Jack Rogers hail from Washington State and compete as the Car Dogs Barbecue Team. In 2002, they won third overall, and placed second in salmon (with this recipe) at the Pacific Northwest Regional Championships, at the Red Hook Brewery in Woodinville, Washington. In 1999, they won a Reserve Champion ribbon at the Canadian BBQ Championship at New Westminster, British Columbia, with this salmon recipe.

3 pounds fresh fillet of salmon (preferably
sockeye or king), boned

FIRST RUB

1 cup light brown or turbinado sugar
$\frac{1}{2}$ cup noniodized salt
6 tablespoons garlic salt
6 tablespoons onion salt
1 tablespoon dried dill weed
1 tablespoon dried summer savory
2 teaspoons dried tarragon

SECOND RUB

$\frac{1}{4}$ cup light brown or turbinado sugar
1 tablespoon granulated garlic
1 tablespoon granulated onion
1 teaspoon dried summer savory
1 teaspoon dried tarragon

Bone the salmon fillet using tweezers or needle-nose pliers. Do not remove the skin. Place in a glass or stainless-steel pan.

Mix all the first rub ingredients in a small bowl and pack them on the

68

flesh side of the fillet. *Do not rub them in*. Let the fillet rest for 3 hours. You will see how the rub has drawn out liquid from the fillet. Rinse the fillet in cool, clean water to remove the dry rub and pat the fish dry. Allow it to dry for about 30 minutes until the flesh becomes tacky.

Mix up the second rub in a small bowl and set it aside.

Heat your barbecue grill to medium or medium high (300° to 400°F). On a charcoal grill, sprinkle wood chips on the coals just before you put the fish on the grill. If using gas, you can put an aluminum foil packet containing fruitwood, in which you've poked holes, on the burners to add smoke flavor to the grilled fish.

Sprinkle the finishing rub on both sides of the fillet (twice what you would use if you were heavily salting and peppering). Place on a well-oiled grill and cook with the barbecue lid closed until the temperature in the thickest part of the fillet reaches 155°F (about 10 minutes).

Serves 4

A fire-heated skewer adds presentation marks to a smoked salmon contestant.

CHRIS AND COLETTE'S VENETIAN STUFFED CALAMARI

Chris Browne and Colette LeGrand

This recipe was picked up on a trip to Venice, Italy, by two young people during a summer of budget travel around Europe, and prepared superbly by the young chefs for their parents, who weren't able to travel.

1 pound calamari (squid),
   approximately 8 medium
1 tablespoon salt
1 tablespoon olive oil

STUFFING

70

4 tablespoons extra virgin olive oil
4 garlic cloves, finely chopped
$\frac{1}{2}$ cup finely chopped sun-dried tomatoes
1 cup toasted bread crumbs
1 teaspoon dried thyme
1 teaspoon dried oregano
1 teaspoon dried summer savory
4 green onions, chopped
$\frac{1}{4}$ cup chopped fresh basil leaves
Extra virgin olive oil
Salt and pepper to taste

Clean the calamari, removing the tentacles, leaving the bodies whole. Place the calamari tubes and tentacles in a large pot and cover with water. Add the salt and olive oil to the water and bring it to a boil over high heat. Cook the squid until quite tender, approximately 1 hour. Drain and cool.

Heat the 4 tablespoons olive oil in a medium sauté pan over medium-high heat until it just begins to smoke, and then add the garlic and tomatoes and cook until the garlic is golden brown, about 30 seconds. Do not overcook or the garlic will be bitter. Lower the heat to medium. Add the bread crumbs, thyme, oregano, savory, green onions, and basil leaves, and continue cooking, stirring occasionally, until well mixed and heated through, or 2 to 3 minutes.

Place the oiled grill over medium-hot (450° to 500°F) charcoal, gas, or briquette coals.

Stuff the cooled calamari bodies with the bread crumb–herb mixture, brush the stuffed calamari and tentacles with olive oil, season with salt and pepper, and grill until nicely charred, about 5 minutes per side (less time for the tentacles).

Serves 4

CEDAR PLANK SWORDFISH WITH PINEAPPLE SALSA

Harry Aldrich, Portland, Oregon

Harry is president of Outdoor Gourmet, makers of the Oregon Cedar Grill Cedar planks, which are available through their website: www.outdoorgourmet.com.

1 tablespoon lime juice

2 garlic cloves, minced

4 swordfish steaks

$\frac{1}{2}$ teaspoon chili powder or ground black pepper

Olive oil

Pineapple Salsa (see recipe below)

You will need one or two cedar planks (available at food or seafood stores, or over the Internet, *not* your local lumberyard). One plank should hold all 4 swordfish steaks. If they don't fit, you can cook the fish at the same time on two planks on the grill, side by side. See "Plankin' It" (page 142) for tips and precautions about cedar plank grilling. Soak the cedar plank(s) in warm water for 20 minutes.

Prepare the coals in the grill to 450° to 500°F. Combine the lime juice and garlic in a large Pyrex dish. Dip the swordfish in the mixture. Let it marinate for 12 minutes (6 minutes per side). Sprinkle with the chili powder. Drain the fish. Gently brush the plank with olive oil, place the fish on it, and place the plank on the grill over the coals, briquettes, or low flame. Grill until just opaque in the center and still very moist, about 20 minutes. Do not turn the fish on the plank.

Planks may start to smolder, but that is okay. But in case they flame up, have a spray bottle of water handy to discourage the open flames. The bottom of the plank will be charred after cooking. Throw the planks away after using, as there is no safe way to thoroughly clean them for reuse.

Serve the steaks with pineapple salsa.

Serves 4

72

PINEAPPLE SALSA

$\frac{1}{2}$ cup chopped fresh pineapple

$\frac{1}{4}$ cup finely chopped red bell pepper

1 green onion, thinly sliced

2 tablespoons lime juice

$\frac{1}{2}$ jalapeño pepper, seeded and minced

1 tablespoon chopped fresh cilantro or fresh basil

Place all the ingredients in a bowl and blend well. Serve the salsa at room temperature.

Makes 1 cup

CRUMBLY BBQ RAINBOW TROUT

3 pounds rainbow trout or other local fresh
  variety of trout

1 cup heavy cream

2 egg yolks

1 cup bread crumbs

1 cup cornmeal

1 teaspoon plus a pinch of garlic powder

1 teaspoon plus a dash of summer savory

1 teaspoon dried basil

1 teaspoon dried marjoram

2 to 3 small pats of butter (2 tablespoons)

Sea salt to taste

Lemon pepper to taste

6 to 8 lemon quarters

$\frac{1}{4}$ cup melted butter

73

Clean and pat the whole trout dry. Mix the cream and egg yolks together and soak the fish in the mixture for 5 minutes. Mix the bread crumbs, cornmeal, garlic powder, savory, basil, and marjoram in a flat Pyrex dish. Remove the fish from the cream mixture, drain slightly, and roll in bread-crumb-cornmeal-herb mixture.

Carefully put the breaded fish back in the cream and repeat soaking for an additional 5 minutes. Remove and gently roll the fish in the dry ingredients again, pressing the mixture into the fish. Place the butter inside the cavity in 2 to 3 pieces. Sprinkle with a dash of summer savory and a pinch of garlic powder.

Place the fish on a very hot grill (450° to 500°F) that has been oiled or sprayed with nonstick spray. Salt and pepper liberally. Cook for 3 to 4 minutes, or until the fish flakes easily, then using two spatulas (*not* tongs), gently turn the fish over and grill for 3 to 4 minutes on the other side. (If using a smoker, put the fish in the hottest part of the smoker and cook for 5 to 6 minutes per side, or until the fish flakes easily.)

Remove the fish from the grill and place on a cutting board. Cut down the back of the fish with a very sharp knife and gently separate the halves, pulling the backbone and rib bones away from the bottom layer. Divide each half. Serve with fresh lemon quarters and melted butter.

Serves 4

DUNGENESS CRAB CAKES WITH BASIL MAYONNAISE

Serve the crab cakes with chilled basil mayonnaise, sprinkled with paprika.

MAYONNAISE

1 bunch cleaned basil leaves

$1\frac{1}{2}$ cups mayonnaise

2 teaspoons yellow mustard or Dijon mustard

2 teaspoons fresh lemon juice

Pinch of cayenne pepper

CRAB CAKES

2 tablespoons olive oil

2 celery stalks, finely minced

$\frac{2}{3}$ cup finely chopped sweet onion

1 pound fresh Dungeness crabmeat (or local variety)

$2\frac{2}{3}$ cups dried bread crumbs, fresh if possible

$\frac{1}{4}$ cup chopped chives

2 tablespoons chopped parsley

Salt and pepper to taste

6 tablespoons flour

3 large eggs

2 tablespoons extra virgin olive oil

Paprika

Finely chop the basil leaves and mix into 1 cup of the mayonnaise, then add the mustard, lemon juice, and cayenne. Refrigerate.

Heat the olive oil in a large cast-iron skillet over a hot (400° to 500°F) grill. Add the celery and onion, and sauté until tender, about 10 minutes.

Place the crabmeat into a large bowl. Add $\frac{2}{3}$ cup of the bread crumbs, chives, parsley, and the remaining $\frac{1}{2}$ cup mayonnaise. Add salt and pepper. Form into twelve $2\frac{1}{2}$-inch cakes, using $\frac{1}{3}$ cup crab mixture for each.

Place the flour in a small bowl. Whisk the eggs in another bowl. Place the remaining 2 cups bread crumbs in a third bowl. Dip each crab cake in flour, then eggs, then bread crumbs, patting the crumbs softly so they are well adhered.

Heat the olive oil in a cast-iron skillet over a medium-hot grill (450° to 500°F). Cook the crab cakes until golden on each side, adding more oil as required. Sprinkle with paprika and serve.

Serves 6

GRILLED MUSSELS WITH SPICY FISH SAUCE

2 pounds fresh mussels

2 garlic cloves, finely minced

$\frac{1}{2}$ teaspoon red pepper flakes

3 tablespoons lemon juice

1 teaspoon lemon zest granules (see Note)

3 tablespoons Thai fish sauce

2 teaspoons brown sugar

3 tablespoons water

Clean and scrub the mussels; drain very well.

While the mussels are draining, blend the garlic and pepper flakes into a paste and add the lemon juice, lemon zest granules, fish sauce, brown sugar, and water.

Preheat the barbecue grill to high (500° to 600°F). Place the clean, dry mussels in a single layer on the hot grill. Grill the mussels just until they are all open and aromatic.

Remove them from the grill with long tongs and serve. Spoon 1 teaspoon of sauce into each open mussel, serving the remaining sauce as a dip.

Note: Lemon zest granules are available from the Oregon Spice Company (www.oregonspice.com) or check your local specialty food store.

Serves 4 to 6

HONEYDEW GRILLED AHI

6 tuna steaks, each 1 inch thick
$\frac{1}{4}$ cup olive oil
2 tablespoons garlic powder
2 teaspoons sugar
2 teaspoons freshly ground black pepper

HONEYDEW ONION RELISH

$\frac{3}{4}$ cup finely chopped honeydew melon
$\frac{1}{4}$ cup minced sweet onion
2 tablespoons chopped green onions;
   use the top green half of the onion
2 tablespoons extra virgin olive oil
1 teaspoon finely chopped lemon zest
1 tablespoon finely chopped mint leaves
1 tablespoon lime juice
2 tablespoons finely minced red and
   yellow bell peppers
Salt and pepper to taste

78

Brush the steaks with the olive oil. Mix together the garlic powder, sugar, and pepper, then season the ahi steaks with the mixture. Dry-marinate the steaks for an hour.

Put the steaks on a heated (400° to 450°F) and oiled grill, cooking for 5 minutes per side. Red tuna turns very white when cooked. The inside should still be red or very pink, and should be quite moist.

Combine all the relish ingredients in a small bowl. Gently warm in a small saucepan over low heat until the mixture reaches approximately 120°F. Spoon the warmed relish over the tuna steaks or serve on the side of each plate.

Serves 6

LES BURDEN'S AWESOME SHRIMP AND SCALLOPS

This marinade gets rave reviews from everyone. It started with a recipe from Hawaiian restaurateur Sam Choy. It was good, but nothing earth shattering, so Les altered the amounts of ginger, garlic, and pepper flakes; added green onions and vinegar; and left out the sugar. Those slight changes made all the difference in the world. Les is the former host of a TV grilling show, writes a column about barbecue, and is a consultant to an on-line barbecue company.

This dish can be served over a bed of rice or mixed in with grilled onions and bell peppers. Allow one yellow onion and one pepper per pound of shrimp.

$\frac{1}{4}$ cup canola oil

3 tablespoons rice wine vinegar

3 tablespoons soy sauce

4 tablespoons peeled and minced
   fresh ginger

3 tablespoons chopped fresh cilantro

3 tablespoons minced fresh garlic

3 green onions, sliced very thinly;
   only use the top (green) half of the onions

$\frac{1}{2}$ teaspoon red pepper flakes
   (more if you like it really hot)

2 pounds (16–20 count) shrimp,
   shelled and deveined

2 pounds (20 count) scallops

Mix all the ingredients except the shrimp and scallops together. Pour the mixture over the shrimp and scallops in a shallow dish and refrigerate at

least 30 minutes, no more than 4 hours. Preheat the grill and barbecue griddle plate on the grill for about 2 minutes over high temperature (500° to 600°F) to heat it up. Pour off the excess marinade from the seafood and discard. Dump the shrimp and scallop mixture onto the hot griddle plate.

Stir constantly and remove from the grill when the shrimp have just turned pink. With the scallops, watch closer as they won't change color, but will go from being fairly translucent to being opaque. Take them off immediately.

Serves 4 to 6

MOZAMBIQUE FIRE SHRIMP WITH PILI PILI SAUCE

82

Serve the shrimp with dirty rice (see page 182) and garlic butter, garnished with fresh parsley sprigs and quartered fresh lemons and limes.

PILI PILI SAUCE

4 tablespoons lemon juice, fresh squeezed
Juice of 1 lime
4 tablespoons extra virgin olive oil
4 tablespoons red pepper flakes
$\frac{1}{4}$ teaspoon cayenne pepper
1 tablespoon sea salt
1 teaspoon granulated garlic

MARINADE

$\frac{1}{4}$ cup lemon juice

Juice of 1 lime

$\frac{1}{2}$ cup extra virgin olive oil

3 garlic cloves, crushed

$\frac{1}{2}$ teaspoon pili pili sauce

1 tablespoon fresh cilantro

Salt and pepper to taste

$1\frac{1}{2}$ pounds fresh shrimp, 16–20 count,
   shelled, cleaned, and deveined

GARLIC BUTTER

$\frac{1}{2}$ cup butter

1 tablespoon chopped fresh garlic

1 tablespoon chopped fresh parsley

$\frac{1}{2}$ teaspoon pili pili sauce

Sea salt to taste

Cracked black pepper to taste

Pinch of dark brown sugar

Prepare the sauce in a small bowl, mixing all the ingredients together and stirring well until blended.

Mix together the marinade ingredients in a medium bowl. Put the shrimp into a Ziploc bag, and pour the marinade over the shrimp. Refrigerate for 2 to 3 hours.

Prepare the garlic butter by mixing the ingredients in a small saucepan. Cook for 15 minutes until well blended. Set aside.

Remove the shrimp from the marinade, and discard the marinade. Bring the shrimp to room temperature and grill over a medium-hot grill (350° to 400°F), basting with garlic butter until the shrimp turn white, or 1 to 2 minutes per side.

Serves 6

OL' JEREMIAH'S GRILLED OYSTERS WITH BUTTER SAUCE

1 tablespoon finely chopped fresh chives

6 shallots, minced

$\frac{3}{4}$ cup dry white wine

1 pound unsalted butter, cut into
1-inch pieces

Salt and pepper to taste

24 Hood River oysters (or your favorite
local, fresh variety)

Hungarian paprika

Combine the chives, shallots, and wine in a saucepan over medium heat, and cook until reduced by half. Remove from the heat and cool slightly. Whisk in the butter, one piece at a time, until the sauce is smooth. Season with salt and pepper, and keep warm over a double boiler of warm (not boiling) water.

Place the oysters on the grill of a very hot charcoal, gas, or briquette fire (550° to 650°F), and close the lid. Cook until the shells open, 15 to 20 minutes. Remove the oysters to a serving platter, being careful not to spill the natural juices. With an oyster knife take off the top shell and spoon 1 teaspoon of the sauce over each oyster. Sprinkle lightly with paprika.

Serves 6
(or just Jerry and me on a cold Washington winter day)

84

JOHN DAVIS'S OREGON CEDAR SALMON

BASTING SAUCE

1 tablespoon balsamic vinegar
1 tablespoon ground ginger
1 tablespoon granulated garlic
2 tablespoons brown sugar
2 tablespoons chopped green onions
   (green ends only)

$2\frac{1}{2}$ pounds fresh salmon fillet, boned,
   with skin on
4 tablespoons extra virgin olive oil
3 to 4 fresh rosemary sprigs (optional)
Coarse sea salt to taste
Freshly ground black pepper to taste
Fresh raspberries
1 cup water
1 teaspoon balsamic vinegar
1 teaspoon granulated sugar

85

You will need one untreated cedar plank (see Note). See "Plankin' It," page 142, for tips and precautions on cedar plank grilling. Soak the plank for at least an hour in warm water, weighing it down with water-filled glasses to keep it fully submerged. During this hour mix the baste ingredients in a small bowl and pour over the salmon, which you've placed in a glass pan. Turn the fish once or twice during the hour. Heat your smoker or kettle grill to very hot (550° to 600°F).

   Remove the salmon from the marinade and drain the fish, reserving the marinade. Remove the plank from the water, brush with olive oil, and (if you like) spread the rosemary sprigs on top. Place the salmon, skin side down, on the cedar plank (or bed of rosemary), sprinkle with salt and pepper, and place the plank on the grill.

Cover and grill for 20 to 30 minutes, or until the fish is cooked and the center is still just a little bit rare. Baste quickly with the marinade once or twice during the cooking time. You want the salmon just pink in the center, sort of medium rare. Nothing is worse than overcooked salmon. Nothing.

The board will probably smolder and smoke; that's what's supposed to happen. If it catches fire, douse it with a spray bottle filled with water.

Remove the whole plank from the barbecue and place it on a serving tray over hot pads on the table for a superb presentation. Divide into sections and serve from the plank. If you are careful the skin will stay on the plank as you scoop up the fillet.

Marinate the raspberries in the water, vinegar, and sugar for 20 to 30 minutes. Sprinkle on top of the fish and serve the fish on the plank.

Note: Oregon cedar planks can be ordered on-line from Outdoor Gourmet (www.outdoorgourmet.com), or check your local grocery store for this brand or others. You must use only *untreated* cedar.

Serves 2 to 4

SCOTTSDALE SPICY SMOKED TUNA STEAKS

Bob and Marti Browne, Scottsdale, Arizona

Garnish the steaks with lime wedges and fresh cilantro.

RUB

1 teaspoon ground chipotle peppers
   (1 or 2 dried peppers, seeds removed)
1 teaspoon freshly ground black pepper
$\frac{1}{4}$ teaspoon New Mexico chili powder
$\frac{1}{4}$ teaspoon ancho chili powder
3 garlic cloves, finely minced
$\frac{1}{4}$ cup chopped fresh cilantro
1 teaspoon dried oregano
1 teaspoon dried cumin powder
Juice and zest of 1 lime
2 tablespoons tequila
$\frac{1}{4}$ cup corn oil

4 tuna steaks (preferably sashimi quality),
   1 inch thick
2 cups coarse kosher salt

Puree all the rub ingredients thoroughly in a blender or food processor until you have a paste. Coat all the surfaces of the tuna thoroughly with the paste, wrap the coated steaks in plastic wrap, and refrigerate at least 2 to 4 hours but preferably overnight.

Prepare the smoker or grill by heating it to 225° to 250°F using liberal amounts of mesquite chips that have been presoaked. You can also use a kettle or gas grill and the indirect cooking method (see page 6). Put the soaked wood chips in aluminum foil, poke a few holes in the package with a pencil, and place the packet on the coals or gas jets. Just watch the temperature closely. Wood chips will smoke very quickly.

Heat a skillet over high heat, cover the bottom of the pan with the kosher salt, and briefly sear the tuna steaks on both sides, about 1 minute.

Transfer the tuna steaks to the barbecue smoker or grill and cook only until they are medium rare, or 15 to 20 minutes. The center of the tuna steaks should be moist and pink. Do not overcook, as overcooking destroys the flavor and texture of the tuna.

Serve immediately while still hot.

Serves 4

ZESTY SMOKED OYSTERS

Jennifer Lyons and Stephen Brennan, New York, New York

Serve with lemon wedges, Louisiana hot sauce, and black pepper. Please, please do not serve these with "cocktail sauce"— you'll love the wonderful marinade flavors!

MARINADE/MOP
1 cup fish stock or bottled clam juice
6 garlic cloves, minced
Several liberal dashes of Louisiana hot sauce

1 cup fresh lemon juice

Freshly ground black pepper to taste

$\frac{1}{4}$ cup extra virgin olive oil

$\frac{1}{4}$ cup fresh chopped parsley

2 tablespoons dry vermouth

   (or lemon or orange vodka)

2 dozen fresh oysters in their shells

5 pounds crushed ice

Mix all the marinade ingredients thoroughly. Shuck the oysters and separately retain the oyster liquor and the shells. Place the oysters in a Ziploc bag, add the marinade, and refrigerate the mixture for 1 to 2 hours.

Heat the smoker or barbecue to a temperature of 300° to 350°F. If using a kettle smoker and briquettes, put them on both sides of the kettle, leaving an open space in the center of the grill. Place the soaked wood pellets in an aluminum foil pan on the bottom grill between the beds of hot coals. Try alder or cherrywood for smoke flavor (see page 254 for more tips on fragrant-wood smoking).

Place the marinade and the retained oyster liquor in a small saucepan and bring to a boil for 10 minutes. Remove from the heat and allow the mixture to cool.

Take several baking pans (sufficient to hold all the oysters in a single layer), and put 1 inch of crushed ice in the bottom of each pan. Place each oyster in a shell on the ice. The ice keeps the oysters from overcooking while they are smoked. Place the pans in the smoker or on the grill away from the fire and smoke for 35 to 40 minutes.

Mop the oysters with the marinade several times during the smoking. Fully cooked oysters are slightly firm, but still moist and juicy.

Serves 4

GOT LOBSTA?

The delicious triplets, *Homarus americanus*

That's what the bumper sticker said. "Got Lobsta?" We were driving through Freeport, Maine, home of L. L. Bean and just about every other factory outlet in the world, when we spotted the bumper sticker. A New England version of the ad campaign for that white dairy liquid, the folks around *heah* are poking fun at themselves and the white mustached crowd.

But if there's a mustache with their campaign it's bright yellow. Butter yellow, to be exact. As in bowls of another dairy product, melted and infused with fresh lemon, that are used to wash down a local sea creature. It seems Mother Nature smiled at Down East and sprinkled its waters with literally millions of lobsters.

Hence the lure for my wife and I, and about 98,998 others, as we visited Rockland's Lobster Festival one August weekend. Over and above tourists, factory outlets, and speed traps this part of Maine has one thing aplenty: lobster.

And we're not just talking food here, Bub. There are lobster dolls, platters, cups and saucers, salt and pepper shakers, bumper stickers ("Got Lobsta?"), tattoos, puzzles, hats, shirts, underwear, oil and watercolor paintings, pencil sharpeners, erasers, gummy candy, balloons, kites, and jewelry ("A 14 karat lobster claw charm for the lady, sir? That'll be $89.95 with tax.").

But let us not forget the lobster Christmas ornaments, charm bracelets,

55th Annual Maine
Lobster Festival
ROCKLAND, MAINE

life-sized carvings, man-sized statues, decorated lobster traps and floats, toys, commemorative posters and note cards, golf socks, needlepoint, and even glow-in-the-dark lobster neckties.

Then there's the lobster they want us to eat.

First, you have your lobster stew, an artery-firming mixture of cream (or perhaps only half and half) and butter filled with Rhode Island–sized chunks of the colorful red crustacean itself. Then there are lobster rolls, which consist of up to a pound of lobster meat, mixed with mayonnaise, butter, and a dash of lemon, all crammed into buttered and grilled buns. We mustn't forget, however, the lobster frittatas, enchiladas, fajitas, lobster Caesar salads, fried lobster cakes, lobster tail scrambles, lobster cocktails, pâtés and etouffées, and the fiery tableside presentation of flambéed lobster.

They grill 'em down heah. They fry 'em. They poach and barbecue. They boil and bake them. They stuff them with crab and shrimp, they make omelets that ooze lobster meat, they cook them in puff pastry and dabble on Pernod sauce, they sauté them with marsala and cream, and they put chunks of lobster in buttered and brandied ramekins and call it "thermidor."

They really, really like lobster (sorry, lobsta), down heah!

To show what extremes they go to, we discovered an ice cream shoppe (why do they always call them shoppes when they sell ice cream?) in Bar Harbor, hopefully offering up "lobster ice cream," and a peek in the case showed bits of red lobstery-looking bits of flesh surrounded by otherwise ordinary vanilla ice cream. I ordered the fudge ripple.

Perhaps the most common way locals facilitate the eating of these armored seaside denizens is when they boil them a bright red, and then serve the scarlet seafood with corn on the cob, fresh-baked rolls, bags of crisp potato chips and, you guessed it, bowls of melted butter.

In other parts of the country, this feast would result in very expensive dinners and long notes explaining expensive expense account dinners to the accounting department. But *heah,* in Maine, in August, during the festival, lobster is as cheap as you'll ever find anywhere.

A scant week before our journey to Lobster Never-Never Land, my lovely wife and I visited a posh Seattle harborside restaurant, and just for sport I asked the price of a whole lobster. I was sort of hoping to begin spring training for the following week's Lobster Festival by getting a head start on the gluttony I wanted to practice on Maine's crustacean-enriched coastline.

"The current market price is $39.00," the waiter gaily replied. "Thirty-nine American dollars?" I asked peckishly. "Yes, sir, but it's a $1\frac{1}{4}$-pound lobster," he extolled.

I ordered the grilled Pacific Northwest salmon.

But in Rockland, at Maine's main event, the Lobster Festival, all fears of having to mortgage my house for a butter-infused lobster tail, or a tasty claw, or even a tad of tomalley, vanished into the briny waters.

Reverse sticker shock struck when I tiptoed up to the food tent to peruse the menu. It read: "$1\frac{1}{4}$-pound Lobster Dinner—$9.95." $9.95? Are you kidding me here? A breakfast in New York City the day before cost me $11.00 for a bagel, one overcooked egg, and a small glass of watered-down orange juice!

The gentle sign continued. "Twin Lobster Dinner—$15.95." Twins, like in a

toothsome twosome, as in a double play of deliciousness, like two helpings of yumminess! Wow! Ain't America, at least Homerus americanus, wonderful?

Then my heart stopped as I read the third listing.

"Triple Lobster Dinner—$22.95." Twenty-three bucks for THREE lobsters! Well, this triple hit a home run in my gustatory heart. A dream come true, a life-enriching experience (for me anyway—the lobsters weren't quite so lucky), a culinary and gluttonous milepost was within three paper plates of being achieved.

Triumphantly I carried my prizes to the picnic table, laying out my instruments before me like a surgeon: the napkins, the wet wipes, the knife, the fork, and the lobster pick. The baked rolls placed here, the cobs of fresh corn there, the trio of fire-engine-red lobsters aligned from left to right. Time seemed to stop. A yellow haze descended on the crowd, or was it a bit of lemon that mis-squirted onto my already steamed-up glasses instead of into the waiting butter dish.

I began with a controlled frenzy, ripping the soft shells apart with my bare hands, and sometimes front incisors, as I dug out the precious flesh, bathed the tender fragments in rich unguents of butter and citrus, and relished each morsel as it touched my tongue. In a flash I had sucked out all the juices, gnawed out all the tender flesh, and picked out any tiny remnants of edible meat from the discarded shells. I was a master culinary artist and the table was my canvas.

Now let me tell you, I really like lobster. I mean, to me it's perhaps the best thing the Lord ever intended us to eat. And when it comes to eating I can pretty well hold my own against anybody. But as the final remnants of the second lobster were gliding butterily down my craw I began to have . . . doubts.

Lobster is, after all, a very rich meat. (I know it's not meat, but that's what they call it here, and after all it is their lobsta.) And dipped in bowls of lemony melted butta, one can only speculate what cholesterol damage one is doing. However, by then I threw away all cares, along with a handful of butter-soaked napkins.

I must say, for a moment there, lobsta number three gave me pause. I didn't give up, mind you. No lobster wimp heah. And even though I did have second, and third, thoughts, I looked up to see two little old ladies from Hackensack, New Jersey, ripping up their trio of lobstas like lions snacking on Christians, and their fervor firmed my resolve.

Rip, crunch, dip, gurgle, chew, slurp, swallow, wipe. It was done. A crimson array of several dozen dozen gnawed pieces of lobster shells sat in a woeful pile at my side. A deliciously disgraceful testimony to my ravenous plunder. Evidence of a triple homarus-cide.

A triple! My, oh my, oh my! I did a triple! Now forever, when others brag about their eating prowess, I could stand tall, and a bit wide too, among 'em. I ate THREE WHOLE LOBSTERS at one sitting. In the end there wasn't enough flesh left on any of the shells to feed a microbe. Not to mention a matched set of corn on the cobs, and a duo of freshly baked rolls that had magically disappeared into the deepest recesses of my being. Burp.

But because I am a professional, a skilled master of the culinary arts and sciences, and in deference to my waistline, I have to tell you that I passed on those tempting but calorie-ridden, cholesterol-laden, waistline-expandin' bags of potato chips.

I wouldn't want people to think I had no self-control.

WE CAME FOR THE LOBSTER—AND FOUND GREAT BBQ, TOO

The Maine Lobster Festival began fifty-six years ago and today ranks as one of the top ten food festivals in America. In 2002, over 100,000 people came to Rockland and happily consumed 23,200 pounds of lobster. That's enough lobster that if you placed them end to end they would be twelve times taller than the Empire State Building. Ravenous visitors also chowed down on thousands of pounds of fresh scallops, mussels, and shrimp, as well as several truckloads of hot dogs, hamburgers, pizza, corn on the cob, and ice cream, which disappeared during the five days of the festival.

In addition to the food tent and the hordes of people devouring thousands of lobsters and other seafoods, the festival features a lobster cooking contest; a children's parade; pancake breakfasts; lobster crate races; lobster eating contests; jug, steel, polka, and accordion bands; several tents featuring local handicrafts; a 10K race; carnival rides and a midway; a wonderful three-hour-long parade down Rockland's Main Street; and evening entertainment under the stars by headliners from the pop and country music worlds.

Two special discoveries merit your attention. On the outskirts of Rockland, on the way to Camden, do not miss **Lil Piggy's Barbecue**: barbecue pork ribs, chopped pork shoulder, and smoked turkey as good as we've had anywhere in the country, and at very reasonable prices. They feature six different home-made barbecue sauces inspired by regional recipes from around the country, and all of them are wonderful.

Author Rick Browne and wife Kathleen celebrate a lobster "triple."

The other discovery was the **Maine Luau & BBQ Pit,** an incredible merging of the best parts of a lobster pound and a barbecue pit, located just outside Bar Harbor. Their lobster is topnotch, their ribs are as good as they get, and their Maine-style red hot dogs are out of this world.

A twenty-foot-long ceramic pig.

A stainless-steel armadillo.

DON'T THROW THAT OUT.

A Ford Pinto?

A crazed Kansas City Chiefs fan.

A former fridge.

LET'S MAKE A SMOKER OUT OF IT!

World's largest BBQ smoker.

A retired plastic injector.

A school bus.

A brew and barbecue.

The only thing it doesn't do is fly.

Once upon a time an old industrial boiler. . .

A stagecoach complete with smokestack.

His BBQ is right on track.

Some people's garbage is another man's barbecue.

Fire engine barbecue fanatics.

Pass the Jack Daniel's, please.

LAMB

ASSYRIAN GRILLED LEG OF LAMB WITH POMEGRANATE SAUCE

One 4-pound leg of lamb, butterflied

MARINADE

3 whole Spanish onions, sliced

32 ounces pomegranate juice
(available in health food stores)

4 garlic cloves, chopped

1 cup olive oil

2 lemons, juiced

2 teaspoons fresh rosemary, if possible,
or 1 tablespoon dried rosemary

1 teaspoon dried marjoram

1 teaspoon dried oregano

1 teaspoon dried summer savory

1 teaspoon coarse-ground black pepper

2 teaspoons salt

POMEGRANATE SAUCE

2 tablespoons butter
1 tablespoon brown sugar
1 tablespoon fresh rosemary,
   or $\frac{1}{2}$ tablespoon dried rosemary
Seeds of 1 medium pomegranate

Preheat the grill to 500° to 600°F.

Combine all the marinade ingredients in a large glass, enamel, stainless-steel, or plastic container, and whip with a whisk until completely mixed. Pour the marinade into a large plastic bag (a garbage bag does fine) and put this inside another similar bag. Add the lamb, turning it to make sure it is coated on all sides.

Marinate for 2 to 3 days in refrigerator. No kidding, 2 to 3 days! It's well worth the wait. Turn the bag over 2 to 3 times a day.

Drain the leg of lamb, reserving the marinade, which you will then strain and put in a saucepan to boil for at least 10 minutes. Remove from the heat, cool and set aside half of the liquid to baste the meat, leaving the other half of the liquid in the saucepan.

Place the lamb on a hot charcoal or briquette fire (500° to 600°F), 8 inches from the flame, for 12 to 15 minutes on each side, brushing occasionally with the marinade.

Heat the saucepan containing the remaining half of the marinade over medium heat. Add the butter, brown sugar, and rosemary, and stir until mixed and the sugar dissolves, or 4 to 5 minutes. Just before removing from the heat add the pomegranate seeds, stir quickly, take the pan away from the heat, and pour the warm sauce into a serving dish to pass at the table.

Serve the lamb sliced, with the warmed pomegranate seed sauce.

Serves 10

105

GRILLED LAMB LOIN WITH ZINFANDEL-SAGE-MOREL SAUCE

Matt Pinsonneult, Amador Foothill Winery, California

One 16-ounce lamb loin

MARINADE

2 tablespoons olive oil
1 tablespoon minced fresh rosemary
1 tablespoon minced fresh sage
1 teaspoon chopped garlic

SAUCE

6 ounces thinly sliced fresh morels
   (you can also use shiitake mushrooms)
2 cups Amador Foothill Zinfandel,
   or a good Pinot Noir
2 teaspoons minced fresh sage
1 teaspoon minced fresh rosemary
2 teaspoons black pepper
4 tablespoons unsalted butter

106

Put the lamb loin in a large, flat glass dish. Mix the marinade and pour it over the lamb. Marinate for 2 hours at room temperature.

Heat a little olive oil in a frying pan over high heat. When the pan is hot, add the lamb loin and sear it quickly, browning on all sides, about 10 minutes. Remove the loin from the pan and transfer to a smoker or a grill over indirect heat with a water pan (see page 6). Cook the meat to an internal temperature of 140° to 150°F, or 3 to $3\frac{1}{2}$ hours at 225° to 250°F.

In a small saucepan, combine the morels, wine, sage, rosemary, and black pepper, and cook over medium heat, reducing the liquid in the pan by one-third, about 30 minutes. Whisk the butter into the mixture and simmer until the sauce thickens, stirring constantly, about 3 minutes. Slice the lamb thinly and serve over a bed of the sauce.

Serves 4

HERBED CROWN ROAST OF LAMB

One 5- to 6-pound prepared crown
roast of lamb, chine bone removed

RUB

2 tablespoons crushed dried mint
1 tablespoon crushed dried rosemary
1 tablespoon crushed dried oregano
$1\frac{1}{2}$ teaspoons onion salt
$1\frac{1}{2}$ teaspoons lemon pepper
$1\frac{1}{2}$ teaspoons granulated garlic

107

Bring the roast to room temperature and spray with olive oil. Spray all surfaces of the meat, as this will help the rub stay in place.

Mix the dry ingredients in a small bowl and rub well into the crown lamb roast. Put the lamb and the remaining rub in a plastic bag and marinate overnight in the refrigerator.

Prepare the smoker or barbecue, 225° to 250°F, for the indirect method (see page 6). If using a smoker, make sure there is a water pan in the smoker to keep the meat moist.

Place the roast on the cool side of the grill. Close the lid. Check the temperature. Maintain the temperature between 225° and 250°F. The meat is ready when the internal temperature reaches 140°F, in $1\frac{1}{4}$ to $1\frac{1}{2}$ hours. Medium rare is the *only* way to serve lamb. Remove the lamb and allow it to sit, covered, for 5 minutes before carving. Serve on heated plates.

Serves 8 to 10

Preparing mutton in Owensboro, Kentucky, for burgoo, a rich stew. The Owensboro International Barbecue Festival features lamb specialties, pork shoulder, and chicken cooked in concrete-block pits on downtown streets.

MAPLE SMOKED LAMB SHANKS WITH WHISKEY ONION MARMALADE

A good Cabernet Sauvignon or Pinot Noir goes well with this dish.

12 medium lamb shanks

MARINADE

4 ounces whiskey

16 ounces red wine

1 tablespoon garlic

½ cup maple syrup

¼ cup orange juice

2 tablespoons dried rosemary

1 tablespoon black pepper

2 tablespoons sea salt

WHISKEY ONION MARMALADE

3 pounds sliced onions (sweet onions like Walla Walla, Maui, or Vidalia work best)

¼ cup butter

½ cup whiskey

2 tablespoons black pepper

Pinch of cayenne pepper

Salt to taste

Combine the marinade ingredients in a large bowl. Place the meat in a Ziploc bag, pour in the marinade, and marinate the lamb shanks overnight in the refrigerator.

Smoke the shanks on an oiled grill over indirect heat, using hickory, alder, or pecan chips or pellets, or in a smoker with a water pan, at 220° to 225°F for 4 hours, or until tender (see page 254 for tips on fragrant wood grilling).

In a cast-iron frying pan, sauté the onions in the butter until soft. Add whiskey of your choice, black pepper and red pepper, and salt, and simmer for 15 to 20 minutes. Remove from the heat and let rest at room temperature until ready to serve the lamb.

Serve the lamb shanks on a very hot platter with small ramekins of the marmalade at each place setting.

Serves 4 to 6

PATTY BROWNE'S BROWNED PATTIES (LAMB BURGERS IN PITA WITH FETA-YOGURT TOPPING)

Patty Browne Anderson, Vancouver Island, British Columbia

110

PITA TOPPING

1 teaspoon lemon juice

$\frac{1}{2}$ cup yogurt

$\frac{1}{4}$ cup crumbled feta cheese

$\frac{1}{4}$ cup olive oil plus 2 tablespoons

$\frac{1}{3}$ cup pine nuts

$1\frac{1}{4}$ pounds ground lamb

1 teaspoon finely minced garlic

$\frac{1}{4}$ teaspoon salt

$\frac{1}{4}$ teaspoon freshly ground
   black pepper
$\frac{1}{3}$ cup crumbled Roquefort cheese
$\frac{1}{4}$ cup sour cream
4 pita breads

Using a medium bowl, mix the lemon juice, yogurt, and feta cheese and refrigerate, covered with plastic wrap.

Prepare a medium-hot fire (450° to 550°F) in the grill, making sure the grill rack is oiled with 2 tablespoons olive oil or sprayed with nonstick spray. An easy way to oil the grill is to take a paper towel that has been folded into a 2-inch square and, using tongs, dip the towel into olive or vegetable oil. Then, with the tongs, rub the towel over the entire grill surface.

In a small, heavy skillet, over medium-high heat, toast the pine nuts on the grill until golden, about 10 minutes. Remove from the pan to cool.

In a large bowl, combine the lamb, garlic, salt, and pepper, and gently mix together. In a small bowl, combine the Roquefort and the sour cream, loosely mixing until just combined. Add the pine nuts.

On wax paper, divide the lamb mixture into 8 equal portions. Gently flatten each portion into a thin patty, and spread one-quarter of the cheese mixture over the center of each of 4 patties, leaving a 1/2-inch border. Place the remaining 4 patties over the tops and seal the edges firmly. Press down gently to flatten the burgers. Brush the patties with just enough olive oil to make them glisten. Two tablespoons should be enough for all of the patties.

Place the patties on the grill and cook until done, 4 to 5 minutes per side for medium.

Place each patty into the pita bread and top with a generous dollop of the lemon-cheese-yogurt mix, about 2 tablespoons.

Serves 4

★ THEY MAKE ★ A VILLAGE

Memphis in May
26th Annual
World Championship
Barbecue Cooking Contest,
MEMPHIS, TENNESSEE

SATURDAY, MAY 11, 8:00 A.M.

The mile-and-a-half strip of green grass lines the Memphis side of the mighty Mississippi. A couple quietly walks hand in hand across the grass, enjoying a park where they are the sole occupants.

The only things moving about are the puffy white clouds, and the river. And it is unusually muddy and murky and fast due to heavy spring rains in Arkansas, Missouri, and Illinois up north. Huge tree stumps, logs as big as telephone poles, and branches pointing gaunt limbs into the gray skies, silently and swiftly pass by. Another peaceful and sleepy day along the banks of America's most storied river.

10:00 A.M.

The peaceful calm is disturbed by a truck and flatbed trailer driving across the emerald lawn. Then a twin appears and parks beside the first truck. Almost immediately hordes of people appear and begin unloading the trailers. Huge wood-framed pieces, looking almost like Hollywood sets, are taken off by hand, set into place, and assembled together. Swine & Dine Building Committee Directors Jim Massey and Jim Fields supervise the mass of 2 × 4s, 8-foot-long $\frac{3}{4}$-inch plywood sheets, prefab walls, and floor sections, and they unload and begin to construct the Swine & Dine "home."

2:00 P.M.

At this moment you can still easily walk from one end of the park to the other in less than fifteen minutes. By the weekend it will take upwards of an hour or more to walk through huge crowds, and past hundreds of booths, to traverse the entire $1\frac{1}{2}$ miles of the contest grounds. The framework is beginning to resemble a small house as team members swarm on the Swine & Dine compound.

4:00 P.M.

More vans and RVs begin to appear, thus beginning the arrival of the hundreds of BBQ teams, some with upwards of eighty members, who will smoke and sing and cook and carouse along the banks of the Mississippi in the annual frolic known as the Memphis in May World Championship Barbecue Cooking Contest.

It takes a full day but now Swine & Dine has the exterior of their two-story structure sitting overlooking the river. All around, other buildings are being put together in a similar manner. Some are two-story, others single-story, some fancy, some Spartanly bare, but by 6:00 P.M. the beehive of construction has slowed. The work crews begin to disperse, with only a few dedicated souls still hammering and nailing and constructing. The exterior walls are now up, the kitchen and interiors will have to wait until tomorrow.

8:00 P.M.

As the last volunteers head off for the evening, the sun dips beyond the mighty Mississippi, and twilight creeps over the roofs of the 350 new "homes" that have sprung up on its banks. There are a few smokers already cooking up a hearty dinner for the construction crews, but otherwise the grounds are quiet. The "village" has begun to take shape.

SUNDAY, MAY 12, 8:00 A.M.

Another truck and flatbed drive up, accompanied by two RVs with trailers. Within minutes the flatbed trailer has unloaded a mobile kitchen complete with three large coolers, a 4×12-foot cabinet for dry foods, a double stainless-steel sink, a stainless-steel prep table, and two large butcher block tables, all covered by a huge white tent canopy. The trailers move up and are unloaded to reveal three large barbecue smokers, one big enough to cook a whole pig (indeed that's what they often do). Twin black smokestacks soar above a cavernous interior that is filled with bags of charcoal, BBQ tools, two boxes of barbecue sauces, dozens of multicolored spice containers, and fifteen to twenty large stainless-steel pans. Team members busily unpack and arrange everything on the shelving units that have been set up in the kitchen.

10:30 A.M.

Other crew members, the contingent numbering forty-five to fifty now, are unloading sections of flooring for the patio and the kitchen, both of which measure 16 × 30 feet, bolting each new section into place, while other volunteers arrange the kitchen shelving, tables, sinks, and coolers. Much of the equipment looks, and is, professional, having been purchased at auction from local restaurant supply outlets over the years.

As the crew continues putting together their mobile kitchen, another RV can be seen coming across the park towing a barbecue smoker on a simple open trailer. Seconds later, yet another RV drives over the grass and parks next to another set-up kitchen, where it deposits a brick red smoker, this one shaped like a huge squatting pig.

12:00 NOON

A long caravan of cookers tied onto trailers stretches from the park as far as the eye can see up a nearby hill. Dozens of RVs and trailers ready to deposit every kind of BBQ smoker and grill that is known to man continue to appear on the rapidly diminishing greenspace.

Smokers are unloaded from huge trailers, or the sides of expensive rigs are removed, revealing trailers with built-in smokers, grills, stainless-steel kitchen sinks and counters, and walk-in refrigerators the envy of some small restaurants. Awnings are raised, chairs are set out, tables are unfolded, and groceries are unpacked and either put in the huge refrigerators, or standard picnic-sized coolers, to be chilled with bags of ice.

Tens of thousands of dollars will be spent by hundreds of teams to construct colorful two-story themed shelters, complete with bathrooms, full kitchens and bars, carpeting, chandeliers, mirrored disco balls and ceiling fans, expensive DVD sound systems, and tables set with crystal, sterling silver, and elaborate floral bouquets. Swine & Dine's budget for 2002 was $25,000, collected as dues from its eighty-five members, winnings from other BBQ contests, and sales of their colorful team T-shirts.

To save money, S&D reconstruct their two-story unit. It's built, torn down, and rebuilt every year. Their "booth" includes a covered deck on the top level, and two stairways to that upper level where "night shift" team members are allowed to sleep late above the fray below while the morning crews noisily begin preparing the food in the ground-level kitchen.

1:00 P.M.

After the walls are finished, the floors installed, and the kitchen has been completed, the facade of the booth begins to take shape, a huge American flag is drawn and then painted across the entire front, and a 20-foot papier-mâché Statue of Liberty is hoisted to the top of the structure as part of S&D's "Americana" theme.

Team members Drew and Jayme Armstrong spent over a hundred hours making the statue, and it now sits proudly high above the festival. "It made us feel real good to see people stop in the middle of the festival to take pictures of our booth and the statue," Drew confessed.

Below Liberty, under the 35-foot painted American flag, are stacked bags of charcoal, hickory logs, 25-pound bags of ice, and cases of beer—critical supplies for the long weekend ahead.

What began as a small weekend barbecue event in 1976 that had twenty to thirty teams has now become a five-day marathon of cooking, celebrating, carousing, and culinary excess for thousands of the world's most dedicated carnivores. Aside from contest cooking, Swine & Dine, like most teams, spend a considerable amount of their funds feeding friends, sponsors and their families, and anyone they care to invite into the private parties they hold nightly.

They'll cook up 300 pounds of chicken, 500 pounds of pork ribs, and over 2,500 pounds of pork shoulder to feed the several hundred hungry visitors who gleefully invade their area each evening. The food is washed down with 180 cases of beer and 28 fountain canisters of varied sodas. And the Jell-O Shooter Committee has dutifully made up 4,000 lime, orange, cherry, and grape "shooters," for the adventurous.

Right now the traditional "baloney bullet" is being prepared for the grill. Two 13-pound rolls of bologna are cut into smaller segments, grilled for 30 to 40 minutes, slathered with S&D's own barbecue sauce, and served as the traditional start of the cooking phase of the contest for the Swine & Diners. The village is up. On with the barbecue!

8:00 P.M.

Tom Lee Park is now filled with fragrant clouds of smoke as other teams fire up their grills, smokers, and deep fryers. The grounds are no longer quiet or peaceful, and will not be that way for seven more days, until Sunday, when the last of the combatants fold up their trailers, dump the ashes from their barbecues, put away unused sauces and spices, and resolutely head off for the next Que contest somewhere down the road.

Oblivious to it all, the mighty Mississippi River just keeps rolling along.

The Swine & Dine team's Miss Piggy contestants sing for the TV cameras.

BACON-WRAPPED SMOKED PORK TENDERLOIN

Donny Teel, Buffalo's BBQ Sauce and Competition Team,
Sperry, Oklahoma

RUB

1 teaspoon garlic powder

1 teaspoon paprika

1 teaspoon Mexene chili powder

1 teaspoon sugar

$\frac{1}{2}$ teaspoon freshly ground black pepper

$\frac{1}{4}$ cup yellow mustard

2 small pork tenderloins

12 to 16 slices smoked bacon, very thick

1 to $1\frac{1}{2}$ cups favorite BBQ sauce

120

In a medium bowl, combine the rub ingredients. Set aside.

Massage the yellow mustard into each tenderloin, covering every surface. Sprinkle the rub onto the meat. Wrap the bacon slices completely around the meat, using several toothpicks to hold the bacon in place.

Let the loins absorb the mustard and herbs, marinating in a covered pan for 2 hours in the refrigerator. Heat the grill to 400° to 450°F. To cook using the indirect method, mound the charcoal or briquettes on one side of the barbecue. Put a pan of water on the other side (see page 6).

Cook the meat on an oiled grill above the water pan for 1 to $1\frac{1}{2}$ hours, then remove and immediately wrap the loins in aluminum foil, put them back on the grill, again on indirect heat, and cook until the meat reaches an internal temperature of 155°F.

Open the foil, lavishly baste the tenderloin with BBQ sauce, and set on the coolest part of the grill for 15 to 20 minutes, at which time the temperature should have risen to 160°F.

Take the meat off the grill and keep it sealed in foil until ready to serve.

Serves 6 to 8

HUCKLEBERRY MOUNTAIN PORTERHOUSE PORK CHOPS

RUB

1 teaspoon dried sage

$\frac{1}{2}$ teaspoon salt

$\frac{1}{2}$ teaspoon sugar

$\frac{1}{4}$ teaspoon paprika

1 tablespoon garlic powder

$\frac{1}{4}$ cup honey mustard

4 porterhouse pork chops, 16 ounces each

Mt. Adams Huckleberry Sauce
   (see recipe on page 122)

5 to 6 sprigs fresh rosemary or sage

Mix the rub ingredients in a small bowl. Massage the mustard into the chops with your hands and then sprinkle the rub over the chops, coating evenly. Put on a plate, cover with plastic wrap, and refrigerate for 4 to 24 hours.

Grill the chops on an oiled grill rack set 5 to 6 inches over glowing coals, or a hot gas fire (400° to 450°F) for 10 to 12 minutes on each side, or until a meat thermometer diagonally inserted 2 inches into the center registers 155°F. Remove from the heat, seal the chops in heavy-duty aluminum foil, and let them stand 5 minutes. Serve with huckleberry sauce and garnish with the herb sprigs.

121

Serves 4

MT. ADAMS HUCKLEBERRY SAUCE

Kathy Browne, Ridgefield, Washington

After a long day in the cold rain picking fresh huckleberries on the side of Mt. Adams, we vowed that the day would not be wasted and developed this recipe to go with game, pork, and turkey. Very hard to find, the huckleberry is worth the trouble, as its strong flavor, crisp bite, and luxuriant color enhances even the plainest meat dish.

$1\frac{1}{2}$ cups burgundy

2 cups beef stock

$\frac{1}{4}$ cup fresh huckleberries
   (or lingonberries or blueberries)

$\frac{1}{2}$ cup sugar

1 rosemary sprig

1 bay leaf

$\frac{1}{2}$ teaspoon cracked black pepper

$\frac{1}{2}$ cup cold butter chunks

122

Heat the wine and beef stock in a medium saucepan over high heat until it starts to bubble. Add the huckleberries, sugar, rosemary, bay leaf, and pepper and simmer, stirring frequently, until the mixture is reduced by half, or 15 to 20 minutes. Remove the bay leaf and whisk in the butter, one chunk at a time, until the sauce is smooth and creamy, except for a few lumps of huckleberry, that is.

Remove it from the heat, allow it to cool, and serve warm over pork, poultry, or game.

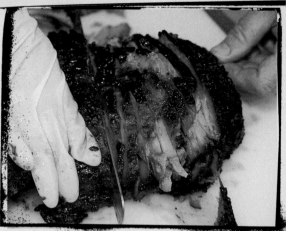

Starnes Barbecue in Paducah, Kentucky, draws standing-room-only crowds for its pressed smoked lamb sandwiches.

Piles of smokin' hot ribs off the grill at the upscale Smokestack Restaurant outside Kansas City.

CAROLINA-STYLE PULLED PORK SHOULDER

National Pork Producers Council

Serve on hamburger buns or hard rolls with a scoop of coleslaw on top.

RUB

2 tablespoons salt

2 tablespoons paprika

1 tablespoon garlic powder

1 tablespoon black pepper

2 teaspoons cayenne pepper

One 5-pound boneless pork butt (shoulder)

BASTING SAUCE

$\frac{1}{2}$ cup bourbon

2 tablespoon molasses

$1\frac{1}{2}$ cups cider vinegar

1 cup water

2 chopped dried chipotle peppers, rehydrated

2 tablespoons salt

1 tablespoon crushed red pepper

1 tablespoon black pepper

2 tablespoons cayenne pepper

Mix the rub ingredients in a medium bowl. Rub the pork shoulder on all surfaces with the mixture; cover and refrigerate up to 24 hours. Prepare a medium fire in a covered grill, with the coals banked to one side.

Smoke the pork shoulder, adding more charcoal and wood chips to maintain a medium-low heat of between 300° and 400°F throughout the cooking time. Smoke/grill until the internal temperature of the pork shoulder is 160°F, or 5 to 6 hours. Use hickory, pecan, or cherrywood for smoke flavor (see page 254 for more tips on fragrant wood smoking).

Mix together the ingredients for the basting sauce in a small saucepan.

Baste the shoulder quickly every 30 minutes during the last couple of hours of cooking; remember, you can lose 15 minutes of cooking time each time you open the lid of the smoker. Boil any leftover basting sauce for 10 minutes, then cool. Shred ("pull") the meat, add sauce, and stir well.

Serves 12

CEDAR-PLANKED SUGAR CANE CANADIAN PEAMEAL BACON, EH?

An incredible cut of meat, this is a Canadian favorite that you will love when you taste it. Try to get it at your local butcher shop, but it is also available on-line through the wonderful folks at The Real Canadian Bacon Company (www.realcanadianbacon.com). The meat comes in 2- to 3-pound or 5-pound roasts. They also sell the world's best Canadian maple syrup.

128

One 2- to 3-pound Canadian peameal bacon
    roast, split in half horizontally

2 tablespoons granulated garlic

2 tablespoons chopped fresh rosemary

$\frac{1}{4}$ cup Steen's cane syrup (or maple syrup)

2 tablespoons French's mustard

2 tablespoons brown sugar

$\frac{1}{4}$ teaspoon ground nutmeg

$\frac{1}{4}$ teaspoon ground allspice

$\frac{1}{4}$ teaspoon ground cloves

2 tablespoons cracked black pepper

2 teaspoons coarse salt

Apple cider in a spray bottle

3 to 4 fresh rosemary sprigs

129

Soak one cedar (or maple) plank for 6 hours in water. You can get specially treated cedar planks from grocery, barbecue, or gourmet food stores or over the Internet, *not* from the lumberyard.

Preheat the barbecue to high (600° to 750°F). If using coals, make sure your hand can only stay over coals 1 to 2 seconds; if using gas, turn on all jets to high.

Score the top of the pork roast about $\frac{1}{2}$ inch deep in a diamond pattern with a sharp knife. In a small bowl, mix the garlic, rosemary, cane syrup, mustard, and brown sugar, and combine well. Then add nutmeg, allspice, cloves, pepper, and salt to make a thick paste. Rub the paste into the meat and set aside for at least 1 hour to dry-marinate.

Place the pork roast on a soaked plank. Put it directly on the grill over high heat for 15 minutes, then reduce the heat to medium (approximately 350°F) by opening the air vents or turning down the gas. Continue plank-roasting for 1 hour. After 45 minutes spray the tenderloin with cider, then cover it with aluminum foil, shiny side down, for the last 15 minutes of cooking. The internal temperature of the meat should be 160°F on a meat thermometer. Remove the pork from the barbecue, spray once again, seal in the foil, and then let it rest for 10 to 15 minutes before carving. Slice into 1/4-inch slices and serve on the cedar plank, garnished with fresh rosemary sprigs.

Serves 6 to 8

GRILLED LOIN OF WILD BOAR WITH SOUR CHERRY SAUCE

1 teaspoon salt

1 teaspoon pepper

2 teaspoons paprika

One $2\frac{1}{4}$- to 3-pound loin of wild boar

1 cup olive oil

4 ounces bacon slices

10 cloves

1 cup water

1 tablespoon all-purpose flour

1 cup cherry-cranberry juice

1 cup stock

6 tablespoons sour cherry preserves

130

In a small bowl, mix the salt, pepper, and paprika, and set aside. Heat the grill to 500° to 600°F.

Trim the meat. Rub with a little of the olive oil and then sprinkle with the salt, pepper, and paprika rub. Wrap the bacon slices around the meat and stick in the cloves. Using the indirect cooking method (see page 6), place the loin on the hot grill above the water pan to which you've added 1 cup water, and cook for 1 to $1\frac{1}{2}$ hours, or until the internal temperature is 160°F.

Remove the excess fat from the pan and stir in the flour. Cook over a medium burner for 1 to 2 minutes, stirring, until the mixture thickens. Gradually stir in the cherry-cranberry juice and stock. Bring to a boil, stirring, and cook for 3 to 4 minutes until thickened slightly. Stir in the cherry preserves and seasonings and cook an additional 1 to 2 minutes. Remove from the heat, and let the sauce come to room temperature. Serve warm with the wild boar loin.

Slice the meat thinly and ladle the sauce over the slices on each plate.

Serves 6

GRILLED PORK CHOPS WITH PEACH CHUTNEY

$\frac{1}{2}$ cup soy sauce

$\frac{1}{4}$ cup sake

$\frac{1}{4}$ cup apricot brandy

4 pork loin chops, 2 inches thick

Peach Chutney (see recipe below)

The day before serving, mix together the soy sauce, sake, and apricot brandy. Pour the marinade over the pork chops in a shallow glass dish, cover with plastic wrap, and refrigerate overnight.

When ready to cook the pork chops, prepare a charcoal or briquette fire and wait until the coals are tinged with white ash (500° to 650°F). Remove the chops from the marinade, reserving the marinade and boiling it in a small pan for 10 minutes.

Grill the chops for 5 minutes on each side, brushing with the marinade, until browned and flecked with brown. The internal temperature should be 160°F. Remove the chops to a hot serving platter and serve immediately, topped with peach chutney.

Serves 4

PEACH CHUTNEY

2 cups peaches (2 to 3 firm and ripe peaches)

$\frac{1}{4}$ cup vinegar

2 tablespoons fresh lemon juice

$\frac{1}{2}$ cup seedless golden raisins

$\frac{1}{8}$ cup slivered preserved ginger

$\frac{1}{4}$ cup finely chopped onion

$\frac{1}{2}$ tablespoon salt

$\frac{1}{2}$ teaspoon ground allspice

$\frac{1}{4}$ teaspoon ground cloves

$\frac{1}{4}$ teaspoon ground ginger

$\frac{1}{4}$ teaspoon ground cinnamon

½ box fruit pectin
2 cups granulated sugar
½ cup firmly packed light brown sugar

In a large saucepan over high heat, combine all the ingredients except
the white and brown sugars. Stir to combine. Bring the mixture to a full
boil for 5 minutes, stirring, then add the sugars and bring back to a boil.
Boil for 2 to 3 minutes more, then remove the pan from the heat, skim the
surface of the liquid, and let it cool for 20 minutes. Pour into a glass container and store tightly covered. Serve chilled or at room temperature.

NORTH CAROLINA-STYLE WHOLE HOG

North Carolina Pork Producers' Association

Pig pickin' has become a favorite pastime for many North Carolinians. Barbecuing pork on the open grill and serving the delicacy from the grill is known as a pig pickin'. Any month or season of the year is good for pig pickin' in North Carolina. Select a congenial group that likes good food and lots of fellowship and you'll have a successful pig pickin'.

Select a pork carcass that weighs from 60 to 100 pounds. A live pig weighing 90 to 130 pounds will dress out as a carcass of approximately the desired weight. The carcass should be lean without too much fat. Excessive fat may cause a flare-up during cooking. The pig should be slaughtered, cleaned, and the carcass properly chilled before cooking.

The carcass should be opened butterfly-fashion for cooking. To do this, saw or cut through the backbone, but not through the meat or skin.

The yield of cooked meat is approximately 35 percent of the carcass weight. Plan on at least 1.5 pounds of meat per person for a generous serving. A 100- to 120-pound pig will serve sixty-five to eighty people.

The barbecue pit should be constructed 12 to 24 inches from the fire to the grill. The advantage of this distance is that it provides more even heat distribution. An easy way to build a pit is using concrete blocks (8-inch) and laying the blocks two high. Build the pit 3 to 4 feet wide (inside measurements) and as long as needed. Lay metal rods across the cement blocks and place a suitable wire or screen over the rods.

The traditional source of heat is coals from burning oak or hickory wood; however, some pitmasters use charcoal briquettes. If charcoal is used it will take approximately 60 pounds of briquettes to cook a 100-pound pig. Start with 20 pounds of briquettes and allow them to burn outside the pit until gray before spreading in the pit. The heat should be distributed so that the hams and shoulders get more heat and the center of the pig gets less. This will allow the pig to cook uniformly. Additional briquettes started outside the pit or coals from the hard wood are added to maintain the proper grill temperature as listed below.

Cooking Schedule	Approximate Temperature
8:00 A.M.–12:00 noon	100°–125°F
12:00–1:00 P.M.	135°–145°F
1:00–2:00 P.M.	150°–160°F
2:00–4:00 P.M.	170°–175°F
4:00 P.M.	Turn carcass
4:00–4:30 P.M	150°–160°F
4:30–6:00 P.M.	170°–200°F

Place the pig on the grill, lean side down (skin side up), for 4 to 8 hours (depending on the weight of the carcass), then turn the pig over. Be careful in turning since the pig may disjoint at this time. Cook with the skin side down for an additional 1 to 2 hours. Be sure to use a meat thermometer and get the internal temperature of the hams to 170°F to ensure the carcass is completely cooked throughout. Remember, do not cook too fast!

After turning, the carcass can be basted with a sauce of your choosing. A typical mopping sauce consists of 2 quarts vinegar, $\frac{1}{4}$ to 1 cup crushed red pepper (depending on the degree of spiciness desired), 1 cup sugar, and salt to taste. Use a new mop to baste the meat.

Enjoy.

Serves 40 to 80

134

PECAN-WALNUT CRUSTED PORK LOIN

MARINADE PASTE

2 teaspoons chopped fresh rosemary leaves

$\frac{1}{4}$ teaspoon dried thyme

$\frac{1}{8}$ teaspoon ground cloves

2 teaspoons minced garlic

Salt and pepper to taste

$\frac{1}{4}$ cup olive oil

3 tablespoons dark brown sugar, packed

One 5- to 6-pound boneless loin of pork

MANGO SALSA

2 ripe mangoes, peeled and chopped

$\frac{1}{2}$ cup finely chopped red onion

$\frac{1}{4}$ cup coarsely chopped cilantro

1 to 2 jalapeño peppers, seeds removed, diced

1 tablespoon balsamic vinegar

Pinch of salt

NUT COATING

$\frac{1}{4}$ pound finely chopped pecan halves

$\frac{1}{4}$ cup finely chopped walnut halves

Mix the rosemary, thyme, cloves, garlic, salt, pepper, 1 tablespoon of the olive oil, and the brown sugar in a food processor and pulse until you have a thick paste. Work the paste into the pork loin, covering it completely, then wrap with plastic and refrigerate overnight.

In a medium bowl, make up the salsa, blending the ingredients well with a spoon, and store in the refrigerator in a covered bowl or container. Mix the pecans and walnuts together.

Mist the pork loin with the remaining olive oil from a sprayer, being careful not to disturb the marinating paste, and then roll the loin in the chopped pecan-walnut mixture.

Prepare a water smoker or barbecue grill for smoke-cooking over indirect heat, with a water pan on the cool side if using a smoker (see page 6 on indirect cooking), at 200° to 250°F.

If not using a smoker, either use a metal smoker box or place wood chips in an aluminum-foil package and pierce with a fork; place on or near hot charcoal or briquettes.

Place the meat, fat side up, on the grill over indirect heat. Cover and smoke/grill for 3 to 6 hours, maintaining the grill temperature by adding briquettes or wood and adjusting the vents on the smoker or grill. Add water to the pan as needed. The meat is done when its internal temperature reaches 160° to 170°F.

136

Remove the meat to a large platter or cutting board, and cover with aluminum foil. Let the tenderloin rest for 15 minutes before slicing. Serve at room temperature with cooled, but not cold, salsa on the side.

Serves 6 to 8

Eesti Barbecue Assotsiatsioon
Estonian National Barbecue Association

ROAST SUCKLING PIG

1 young suckling pig, 20 to 25 pounds
2½ cups white vinegar
5 gallons very cold water (or enough to cover pig)

STUFFING

3 cups bread crumbs
2 cups chopped onions
1 cup chopped celery
1½ cups chopped apples
1 cup chopped apricots
¼ cup ground sage
¼ cup salt
⅛ cup pepper

137

BASTING SAUCE

1 cup honey
1 cup soy sauce
1 cup orange juice
2 limes, cut in slices
2 lemons, cut in slices
1 tablespoon salt

2 cups chicken stock
1 cup dry white wine

Wash the pig inside and out and soak it in the vinegar and water solution (½ cup vinegar to 1 gallon water) for a few hours. Weigh the pig down so it is completely submerged. This freshens and whitens the meat.

Place the stuffing ingredients in a large bowl and hand toss to mix thoroughly. Firmly fill the stomach cavity with stuffing and season with sage, salt, and pepper. This not only adds a tasty side dish, but keeps the pig from collapsing in on itself during cooking.

The easiest way to close the opening in the pig is to use an ice pick or an upholstery needle to punch rows of holes about an inch apart on both sides of the stomach flaps. Then lace it up with thick string just as you would a shoe. You may also use skewers and string as you would for a turkey, or just thread a long skewer from side to side, closing the opening.

Because protein firms as it cooks, the pig will stay in whatever position you place it. It should resemble a dog resting on its haunches. Place the pig on the grill. If it is too large, it may have to be placed diagonally. Tuck the hind legs close to the stomach on either side; tie them together with string under the stomach if needed. The forelegs should be pointing straight ahead (also tied together so they won't spread out), with the head resting between them.

Mix the basting sauce ingredients in a large pan over medium-high and heat until well mixed, about 5 minutes.

Tear off small bits of aluminum foil and fit foil caps over the ears, snout, and tail to prevent burning. These caps should be removed about 30 minutes before the barbecue is completed to obtain a uniform baking color. Place a wooden block or round stone in the pig's mouth, so that a red apple, or other fruit, can be inserted when the barbecue is completed.

Briquettes are placed only on the sides of the charcoal grill and are separated from the suckling pig by the walls of the foil drip pan. To make this drip pan, use 3 sheets of heavy aluminum foil, molded slightly larger than the pig, to collect the rich drippings. Place the cooking grill over the foil drip pan. This will allow you to add more briquettes as needed, and to collect the basting fluids. All cooking is done by reflected heat, not by direct flame.

Place about 35 briquettes on each side of the foil drip pan and ignite. It will take 25 to 30 minutes for the briquettes to be ready for the cooking to begin. Place a meat thermometer in the pig, being careful not to hit the bone, which would reflect an incorrect reading. Approximate cooking time will be 10 minutes per pound of body weight. For a pig of 30 pounds, this is about 5 hours. The thermometer will read 160° to 170°F when the suckling pig is done. During cooking baste the pig with a long mop or brush about once an hour.

The barbecue should be operating with all dampers wide open, and the addition of approximately 12 briquettes to each side every $1\frac{1}{2}$ hours will be necessary. About 30 minutes before the suckling pig is done, baste generously with the basting sauce and remove the foil from ears, snout, and tail.

Remove the pig from the grill to a cutting board and wrap in foil, letting the meat sit for 20 minutes so juices can retreat back into meat.

Make a sauce by skimming the fat off the juices in the roasting pan and discarding. Place the roasting pan and remaining liquid over two burners, add the stock and the wine, and bring to a simmer. Stir to dissolve all the roasting juices coagulated on the bottom and continue cooking for about 10 minutes. You can add wine, orange juice, Coca-Cola, or other flavored liquid. If you wish to thicken the sauce, whisk in 2 tablespoons of flour that have been blended with 2 tablespoons of butter. Bring the sauce back to a boil for 2 minutes, stirring constantly.

To serve the barbecued pig, slice the skin from the base of the tail to the back of the neck and peel the skin down the sides. Carve the small hams first, slice the rib sections next, and carve the front shoulders and jowl last.

139

Serves 8 to 10

And this little piggie went to a barbecue.

SOUTHERN SUGARED RIBS

Carl Triola, Houston, Texas

These are perhaps the simplest and most delicious ribs I have ever tasted.

Salt and pepper to taste
2 racks of pork ribs, membrane removed
1 cup dark brown sugar
Cayenne pepper to taste

Salt and pepper the ribs and put them on an oiled grill rack in a smoker for 4 hours at 165°F. Or you can use the indirect method of heat with a water pan (see page 6).

When cooked, remove the ribs from the smoker or grill, place on aluminum foil, and generously rub both sides with the brown sugar. Sprinkle a small amount of cayenne on each side.

Completely seal the ribs in a double thickness of heavy-duty foil, sealing each layer separately, and put the foiled ribs back in the smoker or on indirect heat for 1 to 2 hours. Cut the ribs apart and serve.

Serves 4 to 6

★ PLANKIN' IT! ★

Charbroiling steaks, poultry, and seafood on a wooden board

Okay, so you wanna impress your next barbecue party? Wanna watch their mouths drop open and stay there when you serve up your barbecue dinner? Then grab a board and head to the grill—we're plankin' tonight.

Wood-plank cooking. This technique, probably copied from the Native American way of cooking salmon and other fish, has suddenly become very popular with barbecuers from coast to coast, and is not only a dramatic way to cook, it also keeps the food moist, adds a wonderful flavor, and is just a plain fun way to present dinner to your guests.

Not only does the wood add a seasoned and unique taste and fragrance to the food, but it imbues it with a smoky flavor, doesn't take a long time to prepare, and keeps the food juicy right up until it's put onto plates.

First, you need a plank (wood board). The best wood to use is western cedar. Alder, hickory, maple, cherry, pecan, and oak are also popular. *Avoid* pine or other resinous woods, as the sap is acrid and bitter and will impart those tastes to the food.

In California, or other wine-producing areas of the country, people have been using oak staves from discarded wine barrels when available. Wood that has contained red wine offers up the best chance of any flavor being imparted to the food.

If you don't want to visit a barbecue store or a supermarket, or don't like to shop on the Web, all is not lost. Just visit your local lumberyard, ask for "construction grade, untreated wood," and have them cut planks 8 × 12 inches or so (to fit easily on your grill) that are 1/2 inch to 5/8 inch thick.

Or, if you do like to surf the Internet, there are several companies that sell

Grilling on Wood Planks.
Where There's Smoke,
There's Flavor

wood planks for cooking. My favorite is Oregon Cedar Grills at: www.outdoor-gourmet.com. That site not only offers the planks in sets of three, but also shares some fun and delicious recipes. Their planks are inexpensive and the "use once and throw away" kind, but there are several other companies that sell reusable planks as well; these are substantially more expensive but you can use them again and again. The only negative factor is that you *must* pre-heat the reusable planks on a hot grill for at least 10 minutes at 350°F to kill all bacteria remaining after the last cooking.

Be forewarned: wherever you get your plank, and whether you use it once or many times, make sure it's untreated wood. Wood that's treated has been soaked in chemicals, which don't go well with food and may in fact be poisonous.

WHAT TO COOK?

Okay, you've got the right kind of plank . . . now, what do you cook? The answer: just about anything you can grill. But remember the plank imparts a fairly heavy smoky taste, so you don't want to cook delicate foods on it that will be overpowered by the smoky flavor.

The best bets are salmon or other firm-fleshed fish, shrimp, clams and oysters, lobster, pork (tenderloin, chops, and ribs), beef ribs or steaks, lamb, or chicken and turkey breasts or legs. Again just about anything you'd grill over an open flame. Since the plank can catch fire, or at least smolder heavily during cooking, I don't recommend items that require long cooking times (brisket, large roasts, etc.), as the food you're cooking may well burn up along with the plank. Stick to fillets, steaks, chops, tenderloins, or other smaller cuts of meat, poultry, and fish.

HOW TO USE YOUR PLANK

If you try plankin' without presoaking the wood, you'll be doing another kind of cooking: incineration, as the planks ignite and burn up that $20 rib eye or $40 salmon. *(Remember if you're using a reusable plank you MUST preheat it at 350°F for at least 10 minutes BEFORE you soak it.)*

Put your plank in a large tub and completely cover it with hot water. Since wood floats, the last time we looked anyway, you must weight it down so it stays under water. If possible soak the plank for 5 to 6 hours to make sure it's real soggy and well moistened. We use large, unopened cans of vegetables or a large pitcher filled with water to weight them down. In an emergency you can soak a plank for as little as an hour; just be careful to check it more often while it's cooking to see that it doesn't flame up.

Some people soak the plank in apple juice, beer, or other flavored adult beverage. I personally think that's a waste and would rather drink the apple juice, beer, or adult beverage. (I like my martinis very dry!) I would hazard a somewhat educated guess that using any soak other than water does nothing to enhance the flavor of the food you're cooking; in fact, if you're using a sugary liquid like apple juice, the sugar may catch fire easier than just the plain wood itself.

When the plank is thoroughly soaked, remove it from the water and rub the top surface (the one you're going to put the food on) with olive or vegetable oil (or spray it with cooking spray) so the food won't stick. Especially if you're using one of the more expensive reusable planks.

Prepare a very hot bed of coals or charcoal, or a gas grill with all burners on high. Preheat the grill for 10 to 15 minutes so it's hot. I actually think a gas grill is the best way, as the gas flames generate a continuous and constant high heat that will cook your food evenly. In charcoal or briquette fires, there are often uneven hot or cold spots that can over- or undercook foods.

Place the food on the plank and sprinkle it with seasonings if you haven't used a marinade or rub. Place the plank in the center of the grill. Close the lid and note the time you began cooking the food.

Keep a spray bottle filled with water beside the grill in case the plank begins to flame, although if you've soaked it properly and you're not cooking something for a long time, the plank should not catch on fire. Smolder, yes; on fire, no!

As the plank heats up and the food begins to bake/broil in the hot grill, two things happen. First, the aromatic wood sends delightful aromas into the food, and anywhere within a half mile of the grill. Cedar is particularly wonderful for this, and that's why cedar plank salmon is probably the most popular plankin' dish. Second, the natural fats, oils, and juices within the food begin to boil and self-baste it from within, creating tender, moist, and very flavorful meat, fish, or poultry.

In most cases, you can go the entire time without lifting the lid to check the food and plank. In fact, this is highly recommended, as each time you lift the lid, you lose precious minutes of cooking time. And when you're only cooking for short periods this can cause havoc with your food.

The plank will eventually begin to smolder, and that's okay. The wet wood should smoke a lot, and that smoke, plus the fragrance of the wood itself, is what plankin' is all about. But if you peek and flames are starting, douse the plank with your spray bottle of water.

Cooking times vary, but the three items we've listed in this book; Cedar Plank Swordfish (page 72), Oregon Cedar Salmon (page 85), and Cedar-Planked Sugar Cane Canadian Peameal Bacon (page 128), come out wonderfully on a plank in under an hour.

In these days of hurry-up and bustle it's nice to fall back on an ancient (some say, slow but sure) way of doing something. Pull up a chair, grab a book and "set a spell" on your deck or porch while the plank merrily does its job. It'll be cracklin' and charrin' and smokin' the way we learned from the first Native Americans, sending up twentieth-century smoke signals that'll tell everyone: "Hey everyone, we're plankin' again!

145

6

POULTRY

BEER-BUTT CHICKEN

The original Beer-Butt Chicken recipe was demonstrated by the author for the first time ever on the *Regis & Kathie Lee Show* in 1999, and about a thousand times thereafter. There is nothing like this recipe for cooking up a bronze-colored, moist, and incredibly flavorful chicken. Not to mention the awe-inspiring way it's cooked and presented.

DRY RUB

1 teaspoon brown sugar

1 teaspoon garlic powder

1 teaspoon onion powder

1 teaspoon dried summer savory

$\frac{1}{4}$ teaspoon cayenne pepper

1 teaspoon paprika

1 teaspoon dry yellow mustard

1 tablespoon sea salt (ground fine)

1 large chicken (4 to 5 pounds)

BASTING SPRAY

One 12-ounce can of your favorite beer; fruit juice, wine, or soda can be substituted

1 cup cider

2 tablespoons olive oil

2 tablespoons balsamic vinegar

Preheat the grill to medium heat (400° to 500°F) for indirect cooking (see page 6).

148

Mix the rub in a small bowl until it's well incorporated. Set aside.

Wash, dry, and season the chicken generously inside and out with the rub. Work the mixture well into the skin and under the skin wherever possible. Place in a medium bowl, cover, and set aside at room temperature for 20 to 30 minutes.

Pour half the can of beer or other liquid you've chosen into a spray bottle, add the cider, olive oil, and vinegar, and set aside.

Take the beer can in one hand with the remaining liquid (half the beer) still inside and insert it vertically into the bottom end of the chicken while keeping the bird vertical as well. Place the chicken on the grill over indirect heat and use the legs, and the can itself, to form a tripod to hold the chicken upright. This positioning does two things: first, it helps drain off the fat as the chicken cooks; second, the beer steams the inside of the chicken, while the outside is cooked by the BBQ heat, making it the most moist bird you've ever laid yer eyes, or gums, on. Some people put a small potato or carrot in the neck opening of the chicken to keep the steam inside, I prefer to let it pass through.

Cook for $1\frac{1}{2}$ to 2 hours. During the cooking time, spray the chicken all around with the basting spray several times. The chicken is done when the internal temperature reaches 180°F. Carefully remove the bird, still perched on the can, and place it on a heatproof countertop. After your guests have reacted appropriately, remove the chicken from the beer can with tongs while holding the can with an oven mitt (careful! That aluminum can is very hot).

Give the chicken one more spritz of the basting spray, then carve and serve.

Serves 2 to 4

BROOKLYN JERK WINGS
(OR THIGHS)

24 chicken wings, skin removed, *or* 24 chicken thighs, skin removed

MARINADE

1 onion, chopped

$\frac{2}{3}$ cup chopped green onions

6 tablespoons dried onion flakes

2 tablespoons ground allspice

2 tablespoons freshly ground black pepper

2 tablespoons cayenne pepper

2 tablespoons sugar

$4\frac{1}{2}$ teaspoons dried thyme

$4\frac{1}{2}$ teaspoons ground cinnamon

$1\frac{1}{2}$ teaspoon ground nutmeg

$\frac{1}{4}$ teaspoon dried ground habanero chili pepper
   (see Note)

1 tablespoon soy sauce

5 to 8 drops Louisiana hot sauce

$\frac{1}{4}$ cup vegetable oil

16 ounces your favorite ranch dressing

Place the chicken in a large, heavy Ziploc bag. Place all the marinade ingredients in a food processor and blend until smooth.

Pour the marinade over the chicken. Do not let the marinade touch your skin; if it does, wash the area *immediately*. Seal the bag, refrigerate for 2 days, turning the bag over occasionally.

Remove the chicken from the marinade with *tongs* (not your fingers!). Grill on a hot grill (500° to 600°F) until cooked through and golden brown, approximately 10 to 15 minutes. Turn frequently to avoid charring.

Serve with creamy ranch dressing.

Note: You can use jalapeño chili peppers instead of habanero, but jerk isn't jerk without this fiery Jamaican pepper—even if it's 1,000 times hotter than the jalapeño pepper.

Serves 4 to 6

CARL'S SMOKED QUAIL

Carl Triola, Damnifino Team, Houston, Texas

I spent a wonderful three days watching Carl and his family cook for the Damnifino Team at the Houston Rodeo and BBQ. I learned tons about "Texas" BBQ and tasted my first deep-fried pork ribs and "frickles," fried dill pickle slices. Yum!

6 whole, boneless quail (see Note)

RUB

2 tablespoons paprika

2 tablespoons garlic salt

2 tablespoons brown sugar

2 tablespoons dried oregano

1 teaspoon ground cinnamon

1 teaspoon ground cumin

Pinch of cayenne pepper

152

Butterfly the quail. Mix the rub ingredients together in a medium bowl and rub on and under the skin, and let the birds sit at room temperature for about 1 hour.

Lay the birds on a smoker at 200° to 250°F, and smoke for $1\frac{1}{2}$ to 2 hours, depending on the heat from your firebox. Or, if you're using a grill, cook the birds over a water pan using indirect heat (see page 6). Grill at 300° to 350°F for 30 to 35 minutes.

Remove from the barbecue and put several birds at a time on a large sheet of extra-strength aluminum foil. Fold to seal the birds inside a foil envelope. Place them back on the cool end of the barbecue and leave for 30 to 45 minutes. The birds will be juicy and moist when the foil is removed.

Note: If you can get boneless quail they are easier to cook, and much easier to eat.

Serves 6

GRILLED TURKEY BREAST WITH HAWAIIAN FRUIT SALSA

One 3-pound boneless breast of young
    turkey, thawed
2 tablespoons olive oil
1 tablespoon McCormick Roasted
    Garlic Montreal chicken seasoning
1 teaspoon garlic salt
1 teaspoon chili powder
Hawaiian Salsa (see recipe below)

Lightly spray or oil the grill rack with nonstick cooking spray, and prepare the grill for medium indirect-heat cooking. The temperature should be 400° to 500°F. Make sure you have a water pan under the cool side of the grill.

Remove the wrapper and netting from the turkey. Brush the surface of the turkey lightly with the olive oil, and with your hands massage the McCormick chicken seasoning, garlic salt, and chili powder into the turkey. Place the turkey on the grill over the drip pan, cover the grill, cook for 1 to $1\frac{1}{4}$ hours, or until the internal temperature of the turkey is 160°F.

Remove from the grill, let sit for 5 minutes, sealed in aluminum foil, then slice and serve with tropical fruit salsa.

Serves 6 to 8

HAWAIIAN SALSA

1 papaya, seeded and diced
1 mango, pit removed, diced
2 oranges
1 lime
1 red bell pepper, finely minced

1 small red onion, finely minced

1 large orange habanero chili pepper,
seeded, and finely minced

$\frac{1}{2}$ cup chopped cilantro leaves

$\frac{1}{4}$ teaspoon salt

1 teaspoon sugar

Place the papaya and mango in a medium glass or stainless-steel bowl.
Cut the oranges and lime in half, and squeeze the juice over the fruit in
the bowl, removing any seeds that drop onto the fruit.

Add the bell pepper, onion, chilis, and cilantro to the bowl. Sprinkle
with salt and sugar, mix well with a spoon, and let marinate for 30 minutes. Put in a chilled serving bowl to pass at the table.

154

LEROY BROWN'S
THAI BBQ CHICKEN

Inspired by a dish I had in a now-closed Thai restaurant on the
South Side of Chicago on a college trip in the 1960s. Best chicken
I'd ever had.

1 can (14 ounces), unsweetened coconut milk

2 tablespoons yellow curry paste, or
1 tablespoon curry powder

2 tablespoons Thai fish sauce

6 garlic cloves, roughly chopped

$\frac{1}{3}$ cup loosely packed chopped cilantro

$2\frac{1}{2}$ tablespoons golden brown sugar

$\frac{1}{2}$ tablespoon white pepper

2 frying chickens, about $3\frac{1}{2}$ pounds each,
split in half

De-Dip De-Dip Sauce (see recipe below)

Combine the coconut milk, curry paste, fish sauce, garlic, cilantro, brown sugar, and pepper in a blender. Blend until smooth. Put the chicken pieces in a Ziploc bag and pour the marinade over the chicken halves. Marinate in the refrigerator for at least 5 hours or, better yet, overnight. Turn occasionally to coat each half.

Build a hot charcoal fire or preheat a gas grill to high (500° to 600°F). Drain the chicken, then arrange the halves on the grill and cook for about 30 minutes, or until the juices run clear when you pierce the leg joint (160°F internal temperature). Turn chicken halves several times during cooking, basting often with the marinade.

Transfer the chicken to a cutting board and cut into serving pieces. Arrange the chicken on a heated platter and serve with the dipping sauce.

Serves 4 to 6

DE-DIP DE-DIP SAUCE

$\frac{1}{2}$ cup distilled white vinegar

1 cup sugar

$\frac{1}{2}$ teaspoon salt

1 tablespoon Chinese-style chili-garlic sauce

In a saucepan combine the vinegar and half of the sugar, bringing the mixture to a low boil over medium-high heat, stirring occasionally for 10 minutes, or until the mixture thickens slightly. Lower the heat to medium and stir in the rest of the sugar.

Cook for 3 minutes, stirring frequently as the liquid comes to a boil. Reduce the heat to low and add salt, then simmer for 4 minutes, stirring occasionally, adding all the chili-garlic sauce and cook for an additional minute. Remove from the heat, cool, and serve at room temperature.

LEXINGTON #1
PULLED CHICKEN

Vicky Bryant, Hendersonville, Kentucky

Serve piled atop French rolls that have been buttered and grilled.

BBQ SAUCE

$1\frac{1}{2}$ sticks butter

$\frac{1}{4}$ cup distilled vinegar

Crushed red pepper to taste

Cayenne pepper to taste

1 tablespoon sugar

$\frac{1}{4}$ cup extra virgin olive oil

One 5- to 6-pound chicken

Salt and pepper to taste

157

Melt the sauce ingredients together in a small saucepan over medium heat, but *do not boil* the sauce.

Rub the olive oil on the chicken, then salt and pepper it.

Cook the chicken on a grill or in a smoker. Grill over medium heat (400° to 500°F) for $1\frac{1}{2}$ to 2 hours until the skin is brown, juices run clear when a thigh is punctured, and the internal temperature is 160°F.

When the chicken is done, pull off the skin and remove the meat from the bones. Feed the skin to your pet alligator and save the bones for a necklace for next Halloween.

In a large bowl, chop up and pull the meat as you would a pork shoulder, pour the BBQ sauce into the bowl, and mix well.

Serves 4 to 6

NORTH CAROLINA BARBECUED TURKEY

Albert Farmer, Bible Baptist Church, Wilson, North Carolina

As the birthplace of barbecue, the Carolinas embrace many rich and flavorful traditions. Many area churches host Sunday afternoon get-togethers. Seeking healthier options to serve these generally large crowds, many have turned to turkey. This is Albert Farmer's original recipe. For additional information contact John Scroggins at (800) 545-4087, ext. 5118, or visit www.eat-turkey.com.

One 10- to 12-pound whole turkey, fresh or thawed
$\frac{1}{2}$ cup peanut, olive, or Canola oil
$1\frac{1}{2}$ pounds bacon, or if turkey is more than 12 pounds, bacon substitute
Salt and pepper to taste
1 tablespoon crushed red pepper flakes
2 cups cider vinegar
1 cup water

Cut the turkey in half lengthwise, removing the back from both sides, and rub with oil. Wrap with bacon (if the turkey is more than 12 pounds, use a bacon substitute, as a large amount of real bacon can cause a fire hazard as the grease drips into the fire).

Prepare the grill for medium indirect cooking (400° to 500°F). For gas grills place a drip pan under one half of the rack, then spray the rack with nonstick cooking spray, turn on the heat on the other half of the grill. For charcoal grills place the coals around the outside edges of the grill, a drip pan in the center, spray the rack with nonstick spray, and light the charcoal.

Place the turkey, breast side up, on the grill rack over the drip pan. Cover and grill the turkey $2\frac{1}{2}$ to 3 hours, or until a meat thermometer inserted into the deepest portion of the thigh reaches 180°F and the leg bone turns and separates from the meat. The turkey should be golden brown.

Allow the turkey to cool. Remove the turkey from the bones, remove the skin, and chop the meat. Add salt and pepper. Sprinkle with crushed red pepper and mix well. In a small bowl, mix the vinegar and water and sprinkle over the chopped turkey and stir gently. Add more water if the vinegar mixture is too strong.

Serves 8 to 10

JOHN'S SMOKY MOUNTAIN CORNISH HENS WITH WILD RICE

John Angood, Saratoga, California

A great, innovative, and creative cook, John Angood has had a tough time in the past year with back surgery. But he's slowly getting back to rare form, cookin' up a storm for wife Kathy, and their precious cats.

159

2 Cornish game hens

Salt to taste

Pepper to taste

$\frac{1}{4}$ cup chopped green onions

1 medium shallot, chopped

3 tablespoons butter

1 cup cooked wild rice

$\frac{1}{4}$ cup chopped pecans or walnuts

$\frac{1}{4}$ cup craisins (dried cranberries)

$\frac{1}{2}$ cup marmalade

$\frac{1}{4}$ cup orange juice

Rinse the hens, pat dry, and season the cavities with salt and pepper.

In a medium saucepan over high heat, sauté the green onions and shallots in 1 tablespoon of the butter, add the wild rice, chopped nuts, and craisins. After the mix is heated through, remove from the heat and set aside until cool.

Fill the hens with the rice stuffing and secure the opening with twine or turkey lacers.

Prepare the glaze by melting the remaining 2 tablespoons butter in a saucepan, adding the marmalade and orange juice, and stir and cook over medium-low heat until smooth.

Brush the hens with the glaze and place on the grill.

Smoke the hens for 2 to $2\frac{1}{2}$ hours at 225° to 250°F. This can also be done over a water pan using indirect heat (see page 6). The cooking time may be less with this method, approximately $1\frac{1}{2}$ to 2 hours; check the internal temperature and when it reads 160°F, the hens are cooked. Brush with glaze before serving.

Serves 4

160

BBQ PEKING DUCK WITH COLD DUCK-HOISIN SAUCE

MARINADE

1 cup Cold Duck sparkling wine

1 cup honey

$\frac{1}{2}$ cup Chinese hoisin sauce

1 teaspoon garlic powder

1 tablespoon ground ginger

$\frac{1}{4}$ teaspoon salt

One 5- to 6-pound duck
Can apple juice
Hoisin sauce, to serve with duck
1 bunch green onions (scallions)
1 package Mandarin pancakes (available at most
   Asian food stores)

Mix the marinade in a large bowl and set aside. Wash and dry the bird, then place it in a Ziploc bag and add the marinade, seal the bag, and refrigerate overnight. The next morning, take the duck out of the bag, drain off the marinade and reserve, putting it in a covered container and either freezing or refrigerating it. Using twine or butcher string, make a loop through both wings and hang the duck from a cabinet, ceiling fixture, or pot rack so the bird is suspended over a pan in the kitchen. Let dry for one day.

Put the reserved marinade in a saucepan and boil for 10 minutes. Set aside.

Place the duck on an upright opened can of apple juice. On the grill the juice will boil and steam the duck from the inside, and the fat under the skin will melt and drip away as the skin pulls away from the meat due to the marinade drying the skin surface.

Heat the grill to medium temperature (400° to 500°F) to cook the duck (on top of the can of juice) over a water pan on indirect heat (see page 6). The water pan will also prevent flare-ups from dripping fat. Use the marinade to baste the duck once an hour during the 2 to $2\frac{1}{2}$ hours it takes to cook the bird.

When the duck reaches an internal temperature of 160°F, take it off the barbecue. Keep it on the can of apple juice, baste once more with a thick coat of the marinade/basting sauce, wrap it loosely in aluminum foil. Remove the can and let the duck cool to a temperature you can handle comfortably.

Cut the duck skin and meat into bite-sized pieces and serve with hoisin sauce, scallion brushes, and Mandarin pancakes. To make brushes from the green onions (scallions), using a sharp knife trim away the roots, cut the scallions into 2-inch-long pieces, then cut vertically into the onion about 1 inch; then, making a cross, repeat this process so that the onion is quartered into a four-segmented "brush." Use the brush to spread the hoisin sauce on the pancakes, add a piece of duck skin and a piece of duck meat, wrap or fold up, and eat. Voilà! BBQ Peking Duck!

Serves 4

BUBBA'S GOT THE MOP
by Baxter B. B. Chicken

The outlook wasn't hopeful,
for Baxter's team that day,
His ribs were dry, his brisket charred,
with one more bird to spray.

And then when one judge gave a six,
and one other did the same,
A darkened silence fell on the team,
who'd sadly share the blame.

A few got up and choked good-bye;
our Carolyn stayed and prayed.
They knew Bubba had entered chicken,
he'd win a prize for that.
For sure he'll come out a winner,
with a ribbon for his hat.

But the Baron had won brisket,
a victory far from small.
And Ol' Willingham said he'd be surprised,
to see Bubba win at all.

And when the smoke had lifted,
and all saw what occurred,
here was Ardie with a second,
while Smokey grabbed a third.

Then from the grilled assemblage,
there rose a hearty yell;
it rumbled through the stockyards,
it really sounded swell,
it bounced off KC stadium,
and off the Stockyard top,
for Bubba, sweaty Bubba,
was picking up the mop.

There was style in Bubba's manner
as he stepped up to the grill,
he had a regal bearing
and a smile remembered still.

And then he fast responded
by raising up his gimmie hat,
the hungry folks around there
saw our Bubba grease his rack.

A thousand judges watched him
as he rubbed away the dirt,
Four hundred of them with sauce spilled
up and down their judges' shirts.

Then while his rivals rubbed their rubs,
and stirred up yet more dips,
the challenge burned in Bubba's eyes,
a snarl spread 'cross his lips.

And now the beer-butt chicken,
came outta the hot air,
he smiled and quickly carved it
with tender loving care.

"Too salty" said one virgin judge.
While from the crowd who waited,
there came an anguished roar,
like the sound of Oscar losers,
as they creep on out the door.

"Grill him! Grill that first-timer!"
yelled someone from the stands,
and it's certain they'd have grilled him
had not Bubba raised his hands.

He glanced over at the judges,
one dressed in baby blue,
but Bubba just ignored her,
as she mumbled, "Hard to chew."

"It's tender," cried his sponsors,
and others called out "Jerk!"
But one gentle look from Bubba,
sent the judges back to work.

The team saw his brow get furrowed,
they saw his shirt get stained,
and they all knew now for certain,
he'd be Royal Champ again.

The frown has gone from Bubba's lips,
he knows it's not too late,
He sprays the bird with practiced hands,
fair Kathy wipes the plate.

And now the bird is on the green,
with clear juices pouring fro,
but the judges are all heaving,
It's not a pretty show.

Oh somewhere in this flavored land
the chicken tastes "jest right."
Ferlin Husky's playing somewhere,
and somewhere gas grills light.

And somewhere smokers bellow,
and hungry eaters shout,
But there is no joy for Bubba,
his beer-butt chicken has lost out.

163

In tribute to Carolyn Wells, Paul Kirk, Ardie Davis, Smokey Hale, and John Willingham, true giants of barbecue lore, and with humble apologies to Ernest L. Thayer's "Casey at the Bat."

7
SIDE
DISHES

ASPARAGUS WITH LEMON MARINADE

1 pound fresh asparagus (choose bright
   green spears with tightly closed tips)
$\frac{1}{2}$ cup melted butter

2 teaspoons olive oil

2 tablespoons honey

$\frac{3}{4}$ teaspoon freshly ground black pepper

Pinch of sea salt

Juice of 1 lemon

Nonstick cooking spray

Preheat the grill to medium high (450° to 500°F).

166

Wash the asparagus thoroughly and peel off the bottom end of the stems with a hand peeler if they seem woody. Place the asparagus in a flat Pyrex pan. Using a sharp knife, cut an "X" vertically from the bottom to about one-third of the way up the stalk.

Whisk the butter, olive oil, honey, pepper, salt, and lemon juice in a small bowl. Pour this mixture over the asparagus and allow the stalks to marinate for 15 minutes, then drain and reserve the marinade.

Coat the grill with cooking spray and place the asparagus crosswise on the grill. Grill until lightly browned and tender, about 4 minutes, turning once with tongs.

Transfer the asparagus to a heated serving platter and drizzle the remaining lemon marinade over them. Serve at once.

Serves 4

AW SHUCKS GRILLED CORN

Try this with sweet white corn, and you'll never want yellow again! If you want to speed things up, remove the husks and place the corn directly on the grill for 5 to 7 minutes, turning several times.

6 ears of corn on the cob, unshucked

Twine, 8 inches per cob

1 cup melted butter or olive oil

1 teaspoon dried dill

$\frac{1}{2}$ teaspoon garlic powder

Freshly ground black pepper

1 teaspoon brown sugar

We usually soak the corn in salt water for several hours to get the shucks moist. (Use 2 tablespoons salt for every gallon of water.) At the same time, throw the twine into the same container and soak it.

Place the butter or olive oil in a small glass dish and add the spices and sugar. Whisk to thoroughly mix in the flavors.

Peel the corn shucks back, one at a time, until most of the corn is exposed and then remove and discard the silk. Do not remove the shucks; they should remain attached. With a pastry brush lavishly coat the corn with the spiced butter or oil mixture, using about half. Reserve the rest.

Carefully close the shucks around the seasoned corn, sealing the end with a piece of the soaked twine. Grill the corn over hot coals or high gas burners (500° to 600°F) on the grill, turning frequently, until done, about 30 minutes. The shucks will often turn dark or black, but they will protect the corn. Carefully peel off the shucks and pass the corn around at the table. Use the remaining melted butter to brush on the corn with a pastry brush.

167

Serves 6

CAYENNE
SOCIAL CLUB

PRIVATE

WELCOME TO ALL
OUR ROWDY FRIENDS

PRIVATE

REEF INDUSTRIES

VERITAS DGC

W & P SERVICES

BFJ
CONSTRUCTION

ENVIRONMENTAL
AIR
SYSTEM

Chill out, folks! It's just a cleverly carved ham—no
felines were harmed in the making of this picture!

BLAZIN' SADDLES FIRESIDE BEANS

John Davis, Vancouver, Washington

John's a big fan of baked beans, and this is one of his favorite recipes. It's great served with beer-butt chicken, fresh cornbread, and a Corona beer. The addition of celery stalks to the cooking beans aids in digestion, and it also can help reduce the effects so vividly portrayed in the movie *Blazing Saddles*.

One 14-ounce can kidney beans

One 16-ounce can butter beans

One 16-ounce can black beans

Three 16-ounce cans baked beans

10 slices bacon, chopped in 1/4-inch pieces

1 large sweet onion, chopped

$\frac{1}{2}$ cup dark brown sugar

1 cup chili sauce

1 tablespoon Mexene chili powder

Dash of Louisiana hot sauce

2 tablespoons prepared mustard

2 tablespoons cider vinegar

Three whole stalks of celery

$\frac{1}{4}$ cup pineapple rum (optional)

Drain the kidney, butter, and black beans; combine with the baked beans in a large pot. Cook over medium heat, on your grill (350° to 400°F), or on a stovetop, for 15 minutes, stirring often until beans are thoroughly heated and beginning to bubble.

In a deep cast-iron pot, over medium heat (grill or stovetop), fry the cut-up bacon with the onion until the bacon is beginning to crisp and the onions are beginning to brown, then add the contents of the skillet, including the grease, to the pot of beans. Add the brown sugar, chili sauce,

170

chili powder, hot sauce, mustard, and cider vinegar. Stir until well mixed.

Bury the celery stalks in the mixture with tongs and move the pot into the barbecue or smoker, at 300° to 350°F, and bake the beans for 1 hour, stirring 2 or 3 times.

Remove the celery stalks with tongs and discard. Just before the beans are taken off the heat, you might want to add the pineapple rum for extra flavor and a nice punch. Remove the beans from the heat, and serve with fresh homemade cornbread or garlic bread.

Serves 6

CAPE COD COTTAGE CABBAGE

In loving memory of Dennis Welch, who could cook up a storm and loved his cooked cabbage while staying on Cape Cod with his wife and daughters many summers ago.

171

1 head of cabbage, quartered and cored

2 strips raw bacon, cut in small pieces

1 small onion, chopped

1 tablespoon sugar

$\frac{1}{2}$ stick butter, cut in pieces

$\frac{1}{4}$ teaspoon sea salt to taste

$\frac{1}{4}$ teaspoon white pepper to taste

Spray a large cooking bag with nonstick spray. Place the cabbage, bacon, onion, sugar, and butter in the bag. Add salt and pepper.

Seal the bag and place it on a grill over a low flame (250° to 300°F). Turn the bag over periodically, every 5 to 7 minutes, to avoid burning the contents. The cabbage is done when it's soft, or 20 to 25 minutes.

Serves 4

CB'S SATURDAY NITE GRILLED VEGGIES

"Ready when you are, CB!" rang the words on the set of many a C. B. DeMille movie, and a young member of the next generation of world-class movie directors is waiting on side stage, soon to walk in his footsteps: Chris Browne, "CB" to many of those who love him. He apparently learned to cook from Ma and Pa.

174

$\frac{1}{4}$ cup soy sauce

$\frac{1}{2}$ cup balsamic vinegar

2 teaspoons dried oregano

1 teaspoon dried thyme

2 garlic cloves, minced

2 teaspoons olive oil

$\frac{1}{2}$ teaspoon black pepper

$\frac{1}{2}$ teaspoon sea salt

2 bunches green onions, use bottoms, including white roots

2 small sweet red bell peppers, cut into bite-sized pieces

2 small sweet golden bell peppers, cut into bite-sized pieces

4 small zucchini, cut into quarters lengthwise

2 small eggplants, cut into $\frac{1}{4}$ inch slices

Vegetable nonstick cooking spray

In a medium bowl, combine the soy sauce, vinegar, oregano, thyme, garlic, olive oil, pepper, and salt, and mix with a wire whisk. Put all of the vegetables in a 2-quart Ziploc bag and add the liquid mixture. Marinate the vegetables at room temperature for 20 to 30 minutes. Drain the vegetables and reserve the liquid for basting, pouring into a small bowl or spray bottle.

Coat the vegetable basket or grid (see Note) with cooking spray, add the veggies, and place the basket or grid on the grill over medium-hot heat (450° to 550°F). Close the lid of the barbecue, and cook for 5 minutes.

Baste or spray the vegetables with the remaining soy-vinegar mixture and turn the vegetables, grilling an additional 5 minutes or until tender.

Note: If you don't have a vegetable basket or grid, just cut the vegetables in large enough pieces that they won't slip through the grill into the flames.

Serves 8

GRANDMA LEAH'S GRAPE SALAD

Tara Bennett, Ridgefield, Washington

A recipe from Tara's grandmother Leah, which is perfect with hot, spicy barbecued meats, fish, or poultry. At first this dish looks a bit odd, but it tastes wonderful.

> 1 large bunch of green grapes
> $\frac{1}{4}$ cup brown sugar
> 1 pint sour cream
> $\frac{1}{2}$ teaspoon cinnamon
> 2 cantaloupes, cut in half, seeded, and chilled

Wash and thoroughly dry the grapes. Mix the brown sugar, sour cream, and cinnamon in a large bowl until well combined, then add the grapes and carefully mix with a rubber spatula.

Serve in the chilled cantaloupe halves.

176

Serves 4

GRILLED WILD MUSHROOM SAUSAGE

2 small chicken breasts, skinned, deboned,
  and cut in large chunks
2 large eggs
Salt and pepper to taste
$\frac{1}{4}$ cup heavy cream, chilled
1 cup cremini mushrooms
1 cup portobello mushrooms
1 cup morel mushrooms
1 cup button mushrooms
1 cup porcini mushrooms
1 tablespoon butter
1 tablespoon finely chopped sweet onion
1 teaspoon dried tarragon
$\frac{1}{2}$ teaspoon dried summer savory
$\frac{1}{2}$ teaspoon chopped chives
$\frac{1}{2}$ teaspoon chopped fresh cilantro
Pinch of sea salt
White pepper
1 tablespoon chopped shallots
1 tablespoon olive oil
Morel Mushroom Gravy (see recipe on page 179)
1 bunch fresh parsley, chopped

Put the chicken breasts in a food processor and process until smooth. Add the eggs, then the salt and pepper, and process briefly to combine the ingredients. Then add some cream, pulse, add more cream, then pulse again, until all the cream is incorporated and the mixture is smooth. Place the mixture in the refrigerator to chill.

Wash and finely chop the mushrooms. In a medium pan over high heat, sauté the mushrooms in the butter until brown, about 5 minutes. Add the onion, herbs, salt and pepper, and shallots. Cook until the onion is translucent, about 5 minutes. Remove the mushroom mixture from the pan to a medium bowl and place in the refrigerator to chill.

Once the mixture is thoroughly chilled, remove the mushroom and chicken mixtures from the refrigerator. Fold the mushrooms into the chicken. Spread a large piece of plastic wrap on a table. Spoon the mixture into a $1\frac{1}{2}$- to 2-inch-wide strip down the middle of the plastic wrap (or pipe it onto the strip with a pastry bag). Roll the plastic wrap into a log, squeezing the sausage material so that it forms a tight roll.

Repeat the process until all of the mixture has been used. It should make 1- or 2-foot-long sausage rolls. Tie the ends of the plastic with string. Gently lower the roll(s) into simmering *(not boiling)* water in a large pot. Poach the sausage rolls for 10 to 12 minutes. Remove the rolls from the water with tongs or two slotted spoons.

Dip the plastic-wrapped meat in ice water to stop it from cooking, then refrigerate the sausage in a wide, flat pan until ready to grill.

Preheat the grill to medium hot (450° to 550°F) and oil or spray the grill. Remove the sausage from the plastic wrap, brush it with olive oil, and barbecue it whole, turning often, until browned on all sides, or 8 to 10 minutes.

Remove the sausages from the grill and place them on a heated platter. Serve with morel gravy, sprinkling the fresh parsley on top.

Serves 4

MOREL MUSHROOM GRAVY

$\frac{1}{4}$ cup water

$\frac{1}{8}$ cup brown sugar

$\frac{1}{4}$ cup rice wine vinegar

1 tablespoon balsamic vinegar

3 tablespoons butter

$1\frac{1}{4}$ pounds fresh morels,
    washed and trimmed

$\frac{1}{4}$ cup minced shallots

$\frac{1}{2}$ teaspoon chopped parsley

2 cups fruity white wine

2 cups chicken stock

Salt and pepper to taste

179

In a large saucepan over high heat, boil the water with the brown sugar, without stirring, until golden caramel in color, or 15 to 20 minutes. Remove the pan from the heat and slowly drizzle the rice wine and balsamic vinegars into the sugar water. Return the pan to the stove, over medium heat, for 2 to 3 minutes, stirring the mixture until the caramel is absorbed.

Heat the butter in a cast-iron pan over high heat on the grill (500° to 600°F) until the butter bubbles. Move the pan to a cooler part of the grill (medium heat), or turn down the gas, then add the morels and shallots, stirring until the liquid from the mushrooms evaporates and the shallots are golden brown, about 5 minutes. Remove the mixture to a bowl.

Add the wine and stock to the cast-iron pan and stir, cooking until the liquid reduces to about 1 cup. Remove from the heat and stir in the caramel mixture, then add the morel-shallot mixture. Stir once or twice and let the gravy sit for 3 to 4 minutes. Taste it and add salt and pepper as desired.

Serve with mushroom sausage, chicken breasts, or beef tenderloin.

OZ ONION PUDDING

Try serving this with grilled steaks or roasts and pour Morel Mushroom Gravy (page 179) over the onion pudding.

8 tablespoons butter

1 tablespoon olive oil

8 cups thinly sliced onions

$\frac{1}{4}$ cup dry vermouth

1 garlic clove, crushed

6 cups French bread, cut into
    1-inch chunks

2 cups grated Emmenthaler or
    Swiss cheese

3 eggs

2 cups half-and-half

Sea salt

Freshly ground black pepper

Preheat a grill or smoker to approximately 400° to 500°F.

In a nonstick frying pan, on the stove melt 4 tablespoons of the butter with the olive oil over high heat. Add the onions, cover the pot, turn the burner to low, and simmer for 15 minutes.

Uncover the pan, raise the burner heat to medium, and cook the mixture, stirring occasionally, until the onions caramelize and turn brown, about 20 minutes. Pour in the vermouth and continue heating until the liquid evaporates, stirring the whole time, for 10 to 15 minutes. Right now the smell in your kitchen will be heavenly!

Spray the sides and bottoms of a cast-iron pan thoroughly with garlic-flavored (or unflavored, if you will) nonstick cooking spray.

Remove the onion mixture from the heat and transfer the onions to a large bowl. Add the bread and stir well. Spread the mix in the cast-iron pan. Melt the remaining butter in a small saucepan over high heat, remove from the heat, and pour over the bread-onion mixture in the cast-iron pan. Sprinkle on the cheese.

In a medium bowl, beat the eggs slightly and add the half-and-half, then pour the mixture evenly over the bread-onion-cheese mixture. Use a spoon or spatula to lift sections of the bread-onion-cheese mix to make sure the liquid is infused throughout.

Place the pan on a barbecue grill and, using the indirect heat method (see page 6), cook for 30 to 40 minutes at 400° to 500°F until the pudding is puffed and golden. If you wish, you can place a water pan under the grill, at the same level as the coals.

Remove the pan from the heat, cut the pudding into large triangular pieces, and serve.

Serves 6

AUNT RHODA'S DIRTY RICE

Rhoda Coles, Hamilton, Ontario

Aunt Rhoda's one of the neatest ladies ever to tease a niece or nephew. Full of life, laughter, and love for every living critter. A very special lady to anyone who has ever been charmed by her impish giggle or her cooking. This recipe came from a family reunion and was a smash hit!

3 to 5 pounds chicken parts (gizzards,
   necks, wings, thighs, backs)
1 teaspoon coarse salt

CREOLE SPICE MIX
$\frac{1}{2}$ tablespoon onion powder
$\frac{1}{2}$ tablespoon garlic powder
$\frac{1}{2}$ tablespoon dried oregano
$\frac{1}{2}$ tablespoon dried sweet basil
$\frac{1}{2}$ tablespoon dried summer savory
$\frac{1}{2}$ teaspoon white pepper
$\frac{1}{2}$ teaspoon black pepper
$\frac{1}{4}$ teaspoon cayenne pepper

$\frac{1}{2}$ cup butter
2 cups chopped onions
4 garlic cloves, minced
1 cup chopped celery
1 cup chopped red bell pepper
2 cups converted rice
1 quart chicken stock or water
2 small cooked sausages, chopped
4 tablespoons sweet paprika

182

Prepare the grill for medium-high heat using the indirect method (see page 6). Put the chicken parts and salt in a cast-iron pot filled with 4 cups water, place the pot in the hottest part of the grill, and bring to a boil, then move the pot to the cool side of the grill to simmer for about $1\frac{1}{2}$ hours, skimming off any scum that rises to the surface. Remove from the heat, let cool, and remove the meat from the bones, chop finely, discard the bones but put the meat back in the cooking water, and set aside.

In a small bowl mix together the Creole spice mix. Set aside.

Melt the butter in a heavy, deep cast-iron saucepan, on the hot part of the grill or on a stovetop burner at medium setting. Add the onions, garlic, celery, and red bell pepper, and cook till the onions are transparent, or 5 to 10 minutes. Add the rice and cook on a hot grill (450° to 550°F) until the onions and rice start to brown.

Add the chicken stock, sausages, and minced chicken to the pan, and place on the hottest part of the grill, making sure the liquid covers the rice by more than an inch. Add the Creole seasonings and bring to a boil. Cook until the water has almost evaporated and is just bubbling on top of the rice, approximately 20 minutes, stirring often to prevent the rice from sticking. Cover immediately and cook over low heat on the coolest part of the grill (300° to 400°F) for about 25 minutes, or until the liquid has been absorbed or evaporated.

Remove the pot from the heat and let the rice sit, covered, for about 10 minutes. Stir, sprinkle the top with paprika, and serve on a heated platter.

183

Serves 4 to 6

SMOKED TOMATO-BASILICO RICE

2 to 3 medium vine-ripe tomatoes
1 cup rice
1 tablespoon finely chopped fresh basil
$\frac{1}{2}$ cup finely grated onion
$\frac{1}{4}$ stick butter, cut in pieces
Salt and pepper to taste
$\frac{1}{4}$ cup shredded Parmesan cheese
1 tablespoon chopped parsley

Cut the tomatoes in half and place them, cut side up, in a Pyrex dish or flat, shallow metal pan.

Set the smoker temperature to 220° to 240°F and place the pan with the tomatoes in the center of the cooking grate. Close the lid and slow-smoke over hickory or fruitwood smoke (see page 250 for tips) for 30 minutes, or until tomatoes are soft but not mushy. If using a BBQ grill, cook using indirect heat method (see page 6) at about 300° to 400°F to smoke-grill the tomatoes over a pan on the cooler side of the grill, for 20 to 30 minutes.

Remove the tomatoes and allow them to cool slightly, then chop into small cubes and add to a rice cooker or saucepan. Add the rice, basil, onion, butter, salt and pepper, and stir. Cook according to the directions for the cooker. If using a pan over a grill, or in a smoker, cook approximately 5 to 10 minutes until the rice is fluffy and all the liquid has been absorbed.

Sprinkle with Parmesan cheese and parsley and serve.

Serves 4

CHIANG MAI SAFFRON-RAISIN RICE

This recipe was inspired by a delightful visit and meal at the White Lotus Restaurant in Chiang Mai, Thailand, during an assignment photographing the Songkran Water Festival for *Islands* magazine.

2 cups golden raisins

4 cups chicken or vegetable stock

$\frac{3}{4}$ teaspoon saffron powder (see Note)

Salt and pepper to taste

1 minced garlic clove

1 tablespoon olive oil or butter

2 cups long-grain rice, Basmati
    or Texmati, rinsed

185

Place the raisins in a medium bowl and cover with warm water, soaking them for 20 minutes. After this time has passed, drain the raisins into a small bowl, discarding the water left in the bowl, and set aside.

In a large pot over high heat, bring the stock to a boil. Put the saffron powder in a little bowl and add 1 tablespoon of the hot stock, mixing until dissolved, then pour it back into the boiling stock. Add the salt and pepper, garlic, olive oil or butter, and the rice. Mix once and then cover tightly, letting the rice cook for about 25 minutes. Please resist the urge to open the lid as every look prolongs the cooking.

When the rice is cooked, it will be fluffy, there will be no liquid left in the pot, and the rice will be easily stirred with a fork. Take the pot off the heat, drain and add the raisins, let sit for 2 minutes, fluff with a fork, and serve.

For an extra bit of color and flavor, instead of raisins use 1 cup dried cherries and 1 cup dried apricots, both cut into raisin-sized chunks. Soak them in warm water for 20 minutes prior to use.

Note: If saffron is too expensive add $\frac{1}{4}$ teaspoon of turmeric per 1 cup of rice for a rich yellow color.

Serves 6

CURSES...FOILED AGIN' TATERS

10 large potatoes, sliced $\frac{1}{4}$ inch thick
5 medium onions, sliced and broken into rings
Sea salt to taste
Freshly ground black pepper to taste
2 sticks butter, cut into $\frac{1}{4}$ inch pats
1 pound sliced Cheddar cheese
2 tablespoons olive oil (per packet)

186

Lay out 2 to 3 pieces of heavy-duty aluminum foil (approximately 11 × 14 inches), and place a layer of potatoes in the center of the foil. Add a layer of onions on top of the potatoes, sprinkle with salt and pepper, add two butter pats, and follow with a layer of cheese on top. Continue to alternate layers until you have three layers. Drizzle with olive oil. Fold the foil over the top and close with a double fold to seal completely. Make 2 to 3 packets like this.

Place the foil packets on the grill over medium coals or heat on a gas grill at (400° to 500°F) for approximately 1 hour, turning occasionally. To check on their progress, you'll have to open a packet and peek. When ready, the potatoes and onions will be browned on the edges and soft.

Remove from the heat and place the foil packets directly onto plates for serving. Caution your guests to avoid the hot steam when the packets are opened.

Serves 6 to 8

TUG BOAT ANNIE'S SWEET POTATO SALAD WITH MARJORAM HONEY VINAIGRETTE

Richard Westhaver, Norwell, Massachusetts

This recipe goes great with any grilled or barbecued fare. When we were growing up, and had family gatherings in the summer, this salad was always on the menu. My first cousin Annie worked on a tugboat in Boston Harbor for a few years while she was in college, hence the name of the recipe.

5 cups peeled and cubed sweet potatoes

6 tablespoons extra virgin olive oil

$\frac{1}{3}$ cup honey

$\frac{1}{3}$ cup red wine vinegar

2 tablespoons chopped fresh marjoram

2 garlic cloves, minced

$\frac{1}{2}$ teaspoon salt

$\frac{1}{2}$ teaspoon freshly ground black pepper

2 teaspoons brown sugar

187

Place the sweet potatoes in a baking pan and toss with 2 tablespoons of the olive oil to evenly coat the potatoes. Cook them on a vegetable grate or basket on a smoker or grill at 400°F for 40 minutes, or until tender. Remove from the heat and put in a medium bowl, set aside, and allow them to cool to room temperature.

Whisk together the honey, vinegar, marjoram, garlic, salt, pepper, brown sugar, and the remaining olive oil in a large bowl. Toss well with the sweet potatoes until they are well covered, and serve.

Serves 4 to 6

DOROTHY'S SWEET POTATOES

Dorothy Browne, Indianapolis, Indiana

Dorothy was a sweet, wonderful woman who could cook up a gourmet meal out of the simplest fare, and who happens to be the author's mother, God rest her gentle soul. I hated sweet potatoes until she cooked them this way . . . now I use her recipe at least once a month, year round.

6 cups water

2 pounds sweet potatoes, peeled and cut into
$\frac{1}{2}$-inch slices lengthwise

$\frac{1}{3}$ cup honey mustard

2 tablespoons olive oil

2 tablespoons melted butter

1 tablespoon minced fresh rosemary leaves

Salt to taste

Pepper to taste

188

In a large pot, boil the water and drop in the sweet potato slices, boil for 2 to 3 minutes, then drain and pat dry.

Combine the mustard, olive oil, butter, and rosemary in a medium bowl, mix evenly, and brush on both sides of the sweet potato slices. Reserve the rest of the mix for basting. Grill the slices on an oiled rack over medium-high heat (450° to 550°F) for 5 minutes, or until fork-tender, turning and basting often with the liquid. Remove from the heat, lightly salt and pepper each side. Serve on a heated platter.

Serves 4 to 6

GRILLED ONION AND POTATO SKEWERS

Serve the kebabs immediately on a bed of fresh lettuce, radic-chio, and sliced onion.

1 pound peeled boiling onions
(about 2 inches in diameter)
1 pound small new potatoes, unpeeled
(about 2 inches in diameter)
$\frac{1}{4}$ cup olive oil
Salt and pepper to taste

BROCHETTE SAUCE

3 tablespoons extra virgin olive oil
1 tablespoon white wine vinegar
1 tablespoon fresh coriander leaves, torn
$\frac{1}{4}$ teaspoon lemon zest
1 teaspoon ground coriander
1 garlic clove, crushed
1 teaspoon wholegrain mustard
Salt to taste
Pepper to taste

In a large pot over high heat, boil the onions in 3 to 4 cups of water until the outside layer is tender when pierced with a fork, approximately 10 minutes, then drain.

Put another 3 to 4 cups of water in the pot and boil the potatoes over high heat until they are tender, approximately 10 to 15 minutes, drain, and cut them in half.

Alternate the small onions and potatoes on skewers. Lightly brush with olive oil and sprinkle with salt and pepper.

Barbecue over the grill over medium coals or gas (450° to 550°F) until the vegetables are heated through, or 6 to 8 minutes.

Meanwhile, combine all the sauce ingredients together in a Ziploc bag. Brush the skewered onions and potatoes once with this sauce just before removing them from the grill. Pour the remaining sauce over the grilled onions and potatoes and immediately serve the kebabs.

Serves 4

NEW POTATOES IN GARLIC-LEMON BUTTER

Pat and Tara Bennett, Ridgefield, Washington,
and their future ballerina/baseball all-star, Alisa

2 garlic cloves, minced
$\frac{1}{2}$ cup butter, softened
24 new potatoes, about 3 pounds, cut in half
2 lemons, cut in quarters
1 tablespoon ground sage
Salt and pepper to taste

191

In a small bowl, using a wooden spoon, mash the garlic into the softened butter until well mixed. Arrange half of the potatoes in a single layer on top of two layers of heavy-duty aluminum foil. Dot the potatoes evenly with half of the butter mixture, squeeze the juice of 1 lemon onto the potatoes and drop the lemon quarters into the mixture. Sprinkle with half of the sage, and salt and pepper. Seal the foil package securely with a double fold. Repeat with the remaining potatoes to form a second package.

Roast the packages directly on hot coals or on a grill at high temperature (500° to 600°F) for 40 to 45 minutes, or until tender, turning packages frequently.

Serves 8

RBQ'S SMOKE-BAKED POTATOES

Slather these taters with butter, sour cream, chili, and/or your favorite barbecue sauce.

8 baking potatoes
1 cup bacon grease, softened, not melted

HERB MIX

2 tablespoons ground sage
2 tablespoons granulated garlic
2 tablespoons dried parsley
2 tablespoons salt
2 tablespoons coarsely ground black pepper
2 tablespoons sugar
2 tablespoons paprika

192

Wash and dry the potatoes.

Rub soft, warm bacon grease into the skin of each potato, covering each completely.

Mix the herbs together in a shallow bowl and roll the potatoes in the mixture, covering completely with the spices. Puncture each potato several times with an ice pick or the sharp end of a boning knife.

Place on a hot grill in a smoker and smoke for 1 hour at 250°F, turning once. Remove the potatoes and wrap each in a double layer of heavy-duty aluminum foil. Seal the foil, place the potatoes back on the grill, and continue cooking for another 1 to $1\frac{1}{2}$ hours until they are soft when poked.

Serve the potatoes in the foil, cautioning guests to watch for hot steam as they open the packets.

Serves 8

UNCLE JOHN'S BEER AND POTATO SALAD

John Angood, Saratoga, California

Uncle John's as good a cook as he is a wood carver, and he's one heck of a wood carver!

$2\frac{1}{2}$ pounds unpeeled potatoes

1 cup finely chopped yellow onions

$\frac{1}{2}$ pound yellow beans, cooked

2 teaspoons plus 4 tablespoons olive oil

$\frac{3}{4}$ cup lager beer

3 tablespoons vinegar (malt or cider)

1 tablespoon Dijon mustard

$\frac{1}{2}$ teaspoon sugar

Salt and pepper

2 tablespoons chopped chives

193

Cook the potatoes in boiling salted water until a knife can be easily inserted (20 to 25 minutes). Remove, cool, and slice into $\frac{1}{2}$ inch rounds.

In a glass or ceramic bowl, mix the potatoes with $\frac{1}{2}$ cup of the onion and the beans. Reserve.

In a medium saucepan over medium heat, add the 2 teaspoons olive oil and the remaining $\frac{1}{2}$ cup onion, and cook until soft, approximately 15 minutes. Add the lager, vinegar, mustard, and sugar, and boil for 5 minutes. Pour the mixture into a blender with its motor running, and add the 4 tablespoons olive oil. Taste and adjust salt and pepper to your liking.

Pour the dressing over the potatoes in a bowl and gently mix. Increase the salt and pepper as needed.

Garnish with chives and serve warm or at room temperature.

Serves 6

★ BARBECUE'S ★ HOLY GRAIL

"It's the sauce, man, it's the sauce!"

Ah, the essence of barbecue. The glorious thickened liquid (sometimes not-so-thickened) that we gleefully baste, mop, and slop with. The delicious mixture we dip, dab, and dribble over our meat. And the fragrant and flavorful concoctions we brush on, marinate with, and slather over our fowl. Oh yeah, fish get their own stuff to swim in too, while they're being broiled, that is!

Sauce. To be specific: barbecue sauces. At the grocery store they come in all shapes and sizes. You have your garlic BBQ sauce, your honey-garlic BBQ sauce, your teriyaki-garlic BBQ sauce, and even your garlic-garlic BBQ sauce.

Colorful, ergonomically and aesthetically designed bottles of magic elixir that we buy by the gallon to give our BBQd creations that final touch of majesty.

In fact, on America's supermarket shelves you have more than *2,000 commercially bottled sauces* available to take home. That's about 1,996 tomato, vinegar, and sugar-based sauces, most using (you guessed it) garlic, and almost all seasoned with salt and pepper.

The other four use the same ingredients, but add special items to make them "different." Different ingredients like Hawaiian lotus-position blossom honey, Tasmanian pink marjoram, freeze-dried Ethiopian cassava root, and Lower Congo River essence of desiccated shrimp.

By far the greatest majority of store-bought BBQ sauces are pretty much the same. You start out with your tomato sauce, add sugar, add salt, add sugar, add pepper, add sugar, add garlic, add sugar, and, if you're really daring, add red pepper.

But how, you ask plaintively, do you find the kind of yellow sauce that you dripped on your new shirt in Columbus, Georgia, when you went on the picnic

What is sauce for the goose may be sauce for the gander but is not necessarily sauce for the chicken, the duck, the turkey or the guinea hen.
—Alice B. Toklas

with Uncle Harold and Aunt Rhoda, or that black stuff they dipped their lamb in when you ate over at cousins Jimmy and Lorraine's in Paducah, Kentucky, last May?

Well, folks, this may come as a shock, but since you bought this book, or someone brung it to ya, perhaps you already know the answer. You can make your own sauce! Right chere in your own kitchen. Zounds, what a concept!

You can, of course use tomato sauce, sugar, salt, sugar, pepper, sugar, etc., or you can go out and invent something that suits your own tastes. Zounds again! Actually zounds like a good idea.

We, the fine folks at this here publisher's place, have set about to offer up a whole passel of sauces you can do by yourself. Sauces that share the rich heritage of the places they came from: Georgia mustard sauce, Kentucky black mutton sauce, Kansas City style sauce, and even Carolina vinegar sauce. Plus we're gonna add a few new sauces keyed to "newly discovered" barbecue regions.

First, we'll talk about the regional sauces that have sprung up during the short history of American BBQ. Going from east (or rather south) to west:

CAROLINA SAUCES: Well, here we have our first problem. Because there are actually several sauces that can be found in the two Carolinas. East of Raleigh you have your vinegar-black pepper-ground-cayenne kinda vinegar sauce. This sauce is slopped on the meat while it's cookin', then served up tableside to pour on whatever you wish to pour it on. A BBQ sauce that's as simple as it is thin.

But over t'other side of the state, you have your Piedmont variety of vinegar sauce. They do it up a tad bit different. They take the vinegar, pepper, red pepper, and throw them in a pot, but then they add ketchup, or Worcestershire sauce, or molasses. In some places they even add a bit of sugar to sweeten the pot. Now you have a red-colored thin sauce.

But then in South Carolina they do it up different again. Around the city of Columbia they whip up a mustardy kinda sauce to serve on their meat, leaving out the tomato, so now you have a thin, watery yellow sauce.

GEORGIA SAUCE: While we're talking about yellow, mustard-based sauces, we might as well talk about the Georgian variety. Similar to South Carolinians, the folks hereabouts think that mustard and pork (ham) go pretty well together, so they stir up a batch using ketchup, vinegar, brown sugar, and mustard to make a thicker yellow sauce. You can't beat this on a slice of fresh ham or a thick piece of pork shoulder.

ALABAMA SAUCE: Alabama's contribution to the barbecue world is a vinegary white sauce thickened with eggs or mayonnaise. It can be almost a creamy yellow color, is not heavy, and is chilled and put on food right before serving. Heating it would break down the eggs. Excellent marinade for chicken, Cornish hen, and quail, and it doubles as a salad dressing!

KENTUCKY SAUCE: Because somehow a whole lotta sheep and lambs ended up hereabouts they have a special barbecue sauce for those kinda critters. They do a "black" sauce, which is indeed black, peppery, and very thin. It's actually a clear vinegar sauce to which they add molasses and sometimes a dash or two of Worcestershire sauce.

In Owensboro, at their mutton festival, they use buckets and full-sized mops to slather it on whole sheep carcasses that are roasted overnight on 100-foot-long barbecues smack-dab in the middle of several downtown streets.

MEMPHIS SAUCE: On the shores of the Mississippi River, in the city that hosts the World's Largest Cooking Event (so sayeth the Guinness Book), they practice a different sort of sauce preparation. They take the molasses from Kentucky, vinegar from the Carolinas, Tabasco from the Bayou, and mix it with lotsa tomato sauce and maybe a glug or two of ketchup. The resulting very brown-red sauce is sorta sweet, sorta spicy, and not too thick.

TEXAS SAUCE: Deep in the heart of you-know-where they like a thick tomato sauce for their beloved brisket. Texas sauce tends to be very thick, the thickest of all the regional-style sauces, mainly because it contains chopped onions. They also throw bacon grease, and/or butter, hot peppers, and hotter chilis into the fray. Sugar is left out. No sissy sweeteners for these cowpokes.

KANSAS CITY SAUCE: There's a good reason KC is known as the "meltin' pot" of barbecue sauces. They use everybody else's to stir up their sauce. They use tomato sauce, vinegar, salt, molasses, mustard, chilis or red pepper, sugar (brown or white), and stir it into a thick (not as thick as the Texans', however) sauce. Most commercially bottled sauces are basically Kansas City–style sauces, as barbecuers nationwide have expressed their love of this thick, sweet, tangy, red style of BBQ sauce.

Kansas City also hosts the only "barbecue sauce only" contest in the U.S. Originally called the Diddy-Wa-Diddy Sauce Contest, it's been renamed (God knows why) the National Barbecue Sauce Contest. Over four hundred commercially bottled sauces are submitted every year to be judged by a panel of twenty-five judges. Sauces are graded like wine from 1 to 7, with a 1 being terrible. Sauces are graded on color, texture, aroma and bouquet, individual taste, and taste on barbecued pork and chicken. The top sauce receives no monetary award, merely the honor of being named the "Best Barbecue Sauce in America."

Traditionally the sauces that we have just described have been the regional sauces of the country—but with the popularity of barbecue from sea to shining sauce, we'd like to add a few more regional peculiarities for you to consider.

CALIFORNIA SAUCE: Californians tend to do things differently, so they have several ways of barbecuing that they've picked up from the Hispanic culture down below their state, or the Pacific Rim cultures west of the state. So far west it's actually the East, the Far East at that!

They cook tri-tip, a triangular chunk of bottom sirloin that most of the country ignores, using a simple marinade, mop, and sauce of virgin olive oil, balsamic

197

or cider vinegar, and finely chopped fresh garlic, which is brushed on the meat on the grill using long rosemary branches tied together like a short broom.

For barbecuing just about anything else, they often borrow from Asian and Pacific cuisines and use soy, teriyaki, oyster, fish, and hoisin sauces with flavored vinegars, honeys and turbinado sugars, and fruit juices (apple, apricot, pineapple, mango, etc.) to make light and flavorful basting, marinating, and serving sauces. Sometimes the same sauce is used all three ways.

NEW MEXICO SAUCE: It's really hot in New Mexico! Not only the weather in the summer, when it can be a scorching 120°F out, but at local barbecues when sun-glazed pitmasters trot out New Mexico–style barbecue sauces to fire up the culinary senses. Cayenne, ancho chili powder, and pasilla chili powder are the holy triumvirate of this regional style. Many of the sauces start out like Texas or Kansas City or Memphis–style sauces, but then the chili powder, raw chilis, and red pepper make an appearance and it's *"Katie, pass the ice water."* (See the Scoville pepper rating on page 200)

HAWAII SAUCE: Similar to California, but more of a sweet-and-sour kind of sauce is popular here. Islanders use pineapple, mango, and papaya juices, both as tenderizers—leave a steak in papaya juice overnight and it's good-bye, steak—and as a sauce base. By adding soy sauce and fresh and ground ginger, Asian five-spice powder, lemon juice, rice vinegar, and molasses, they come up with delicious, fresh, fruity-flavored sauces. Great on poultry and chicken. However, there is *no* BBQ sauce that tastes good on poi.

PACIFIC NORTHWEST SAUCE: Two things influence sauces up in the Pacific NW. First, the abundance of fresh (really fresh, like right out of the Columbia River onto a grill) salmon. The second is the abundance of really fresh berries, primarily blueberries, raspberries, huckleberries, and marionberries.

Addressing the fruit sauces first, there are several commercial bottling companies that make a fantastic line of fruit barbecue sauces. With the predominance of roadside stands selling "just-picked" berries it's easy for anyone to grab a handful, put them in a saucepan with some spices (garlic, salt, pepper, paprika, savory, cumin, etc.), and whip up sauces that are heavenly on chicken, turkey, and just about any fish fillets or steaks.

And, as long as we're talking about fish, nowhere in the country do people have as many opportunities to buy right-from-the-river (or ocean) salmon. And since most commercial barbecue sauces, or most tomato-based sauces, would overpower the subtle taste of the salmon, the folks from Gold Beach, Oregon, to Birch Bay, Washington, have cleverly developed some marinades and sauces especially for this marine treasure.

Similar to the neighbors to the south of them in the Golden State, they use soy, lemon and lime juices, ginger, garlic, dried mushrooms, and fresh herbs like basil, cilantro, and savory to flavor the tender flesh of their Copper River, coho, sockeye, pink, silver, and king salmon.

Well, I hope you've enjoyed your tour of the saucier side of America. We've tried to share the regional specialties that you should try, we've tried to encourage you to experiment, innovate, and cast away all fears as you formulate your own barbeculinary concoctions, and we've tried to get you guys to go boldly where no man has gone—into the Round Table of barbecue sauces.

Buy ye not just the bottled sauces from your local market, rely ye not solely on the Sauce of the Month Club, nor your Mother's ketchup, mustard, and cayenne pepper recipe. Be brave, get thyself to a bowl, cast in tomatoes, and fruits, and spices, and beer, and oils, and sweeteners, and verily we say you'll come up with your own Merlin's brew of Que.

"Hey, Guinevere, pass the Holy Grail of Sauce, will ya Babe? This guinea fowl is like drysville!"

SAUCE-Y FACTS*

Almost nine out of ten (88 percent) grill owners use barbecue sauce when they grill.

The vast majority (84 percent) of those who use BBQ sauce when they grill use it as a basting sauce during cooking.

About half (52 percent) use barbecue sauce as a marinade before cooking. Two out of five (40 percent) use it as a condiment after the meal is cooked.

Hickory flavor is by far the most popular commercially bottled sauce (61 percent).

Other sauces used regularly include honey (36 percent), mesquite (35 percent), and tomato-based (34 percent). Soy-based sauce is far less popular (9 percent).

*Statistics provided by the Hearth, Patio & Barbecue Association biannual consumer study.

HOW HOT IS DAT PEPPA?*

Scoville Units, Chili Varieties, and Commercial Products

0: mild bells, pimiento, sweet banana, U.S. paprika. *Your six-month-old baby wouldn't even burp after a taste.*

10–100: pickled pepperoncini. *If you think hard you'll taste something kinda lukewarm. I've had spicier oatmeal.*

100–500: NuMex R-Naky, Mexi-Bell, cherry-canned green chilis, Hungarian hot paprika. *Wouldn't even melt an ice cube in your mouth.*

500–1000: NuMex Big Jim, NuMex 6–4, chili powder. *Starting to get a tiny tingle when my gums touch this level of chilis. Sorta nice and warming. Sorta.*

1,000–1,500: ancho, pasilla, española improved, Old Bay Seasoning. *Now we're talking! A bit of a flame erupts, sorta like a pilot light in a gas fireplace.*

1,500–2,500: sandia, cascabel, yellow wax hot. *Yes, there is heat here all right, not blazing heat, just a mild incendiary burn to the gums. A tiny blister or two perhaps.*

2,500–5,000: TAM mild jalapeño; mirasol; cayenne, large, red, thick; Louisiana hot sauce. *Taste some and you can melt a glass full of ice, or clear the frost from your rearview mirror on a February morning in Anchorage.*

5,000–15,000: early jalapeño, aj amarillo, serrano, Tabasco sauce. *A bit of fiery unpleasantness for most of us, the edges of my tongue are browning like sautéed liver in a nonstick frying pan. A fifth of Pepto-Bismol, please?*

15,000–30,000: de arbol, crushed red pepper, habanero hot sauce. *Hot, really, really hot. Please pass a gallon of milk, 2 quarts of ice cream, and some cold towels.*

30,000–50,000: piquin; cayenne long; Tabasco, Thai *prik khee nu*, Pakistan *dundicut. You gotta be kidding! People willingly eat this stuff? My mouth feels like the jet engine of an F-14 as it kicks in the afterburner. Mamma mia, my lips have melted!*

50,000–100,000: santaka, chiltepin, rocoto, Chinese *kwangsi. Please, I'll plead guilty to any crime you want me to, only don't make me taste any more. The hell with the Chinese water torture, they should have used drops of this and saved about a jillion gallons of water.*

100,000–500,000: habanero, Scotch bonnet, South American *chinenses*, African birdseye. *My mouth has died. I have no tongue or teeth or throat left. The flames coming from me would start the space shuttle rocket, melt one of the pyramids, and cook bacon and eggs for the entire African continent. Please pass me a fire extinguisher.*

*Reprinted with permission from the Fiery Foods website (www.fieryfoods.com). Comments by R. Browne.

8

SAUCES, MARINADES, AND DRY RUBS

BOURBON SALMON MOP

$\frac{1}{2}$ cup olive oil

4 tablespoons good bourbon

4 tablespoons rice vinegar

1 teaspoon onion powder

1 teaspoon dried dill

1 teaspoon brown sugar

Pinch of sea salt

Pinch of white pepper

In a large bowl, mix the ingredients and stir until thoroughly blended. After mixing pour into a container, seal, and refrigerate until ready to use. If the olive oil has thickened when you are ready to use it, pour the liquid into a medium saucepan and heat until just warmed through and the olive oil is fully liquid again. It can be used as a marinade, baste, or sauce. Especially good on salmon and other fish, but tastes pretty darn good on chicken and pork too!

204

Makes $\frac{1}{2}$ to $\frac{3}{4}$ cup
(good for about 4 pounds of salmon)

CRANBERRY-LEMON BBQ GLAZE

One 8-ounce can cranberry sauce

$\frac{1}{8}$ teaspoon dried, crushed rosemary

$\frac{1}{4}$ cup finely chopped dried cranberries

$\frac{1}{2}$ cup cranberry juice

2 tablespoons lemon juice

$\frac{1}{2}$ teaspoon finely chopped lemon peel

$\frac{1}{4}$ cup honey

In a saucepan over medium heat, combine all the ingredients and stir constantly while bringing to a boil. Keep over medium heat until the sauce reduces by one-third. Remove from the heat and let it cool. Use the sauce to baste turkey, chicken, lamb, or pork several times during the last 5 minutes on the grill.

Makes 1 to $1\frac{1}{2}$ cups

'BAMA BBQ SAUCE

David Donahoo, Prattville, Alabama

1 teaspoon crushed garlic
$\frac{3}{4}$ cup white vinegar
6 ounces tomato paste
$\frac{1}{2}$ cup dark molasses
$\frac{1}{4}$ cup A-1 sauce
$\frac{1}{4}$ cup beer
2 tablespoons orange marmalade
$\frac{1}{2}$ teaspoon ground ginger
$\frac{1}{4}$ teaspoon ground nutmeg
$\frac{1}{4}$ teaspoon celery seed
$\frac{1}{4}$ teaspoon dried oregano
$\frac{1}{8}$ teaspoon cayenne pepper
$1\frac{1}{2}$ teaspoons sea salt
$\frac{1}{2}$ teaspoon black pepper
1 tablespoon liquid smoke

205

In a medium saucepan, combine all the ingredients except the liquid smoke. Bring to a boil over high heat, stirring occasionally. Reduce the heat to low and simmer gently, uncovered, for 20 minutes, stirring occasionally. Remove from the heat. Add the liquid smoke. Stir for 2 to 3 minutes. Let it cool and use on meat, poultry, game, or vegetables.

Makes 2 to $2\frac{1}{2}$ cups

BEER BUTTE RANCH SAUCE

Inspired by the delicious sauce served alongside the blackest, moistest piece of brisket I ever had—at the 2000 Houston Rodeo and Barbecue Competition.

$\frac{1}{2}$ cup white vinegar

$\frac{1}{2}$ pound bacon grease

$\frac{1}{2}$ pound butter

1 tablespoon freshly ground black pepper

1 tablespoon cayenne pepper

3 onions, chopped

$\frac{1}{4}$ cup Worcestershire sauce

3 cups ketchup

1 tablespoon salt

1 tablespoon celery salt

1 tablespoon garlic salt

206

In a large saucepan, over low heat on a stovetop burner, combine all the ingredients and simmer for at least 45 minutes. Makes sauce for a 20-pound brisket or a whole mess o' beef or pork ribs.

Makes $4\frac{1}{2}$ to 5 cups

CHARDONNAY MARINADE

$\frac{1}{2}$ cup soy sauce

$\frac{1}{2}$ cup Chardonnay

$\frac{1}{2}$ cup water

1 bunch of green onions, coarsely chopped

5 fresh garlic cloves, coarsely chopped and crushed

1 small ginger root, peeled and diced

3 tablespoons cane syrup

Freshly ground black pepper

Pinch of salt

$\frac{1}{2}$ teaspoon sesame oil

Mix all the ingredients in a medium glass or stainless-steel bowl. Place in a sealable container and set aside until you wish to use it. A great marinade for beef, pork, or lamb. Can also be used to baste meat while cooking.

Makes $1\frac{1}{2}$ to 2 cups

207

HORSEY SAUCE WITH A BITE

1 cup mayonnaise

$\frac{1}{4}$ cup water

2 ounces prepared horseradish

2 tablespoons Louisiana hot sauce

1 tablespoon spicy mustard

2 tablespoons sugar

Pinch of black pepper

Pinch of salt

In a medium bowl, mix the ingredients together with a spoon and let the sauce sit in the refrigerator for about 30 minutes. It's super on brisket or BBQd roast pork that has been pulled or chopped for sandwiches. Also, this adds a great taste when served alongside roast beef cooked on the barbecue.

Makes $1\frac{1}{2}$ cups

DRACULA'S BLOOD ORANGE SAUCE

One $10\frac{3}{4}$-ounce can tomato soup

1 cup tomato sauce

2 tablespoons soy sauce

1 tablespoon Worcestershire sauce

$\frac{1}{2}$ cup light molasses

2 tablespoons finely chopped orange zest

$\frac{1}{2}$ cup blood orange juice, about 2 to 3 oranges

$1\frac{1}{2}$ tablespoons dry mustard

2 teaspoons paprika

$\frac{1}{2}$ cup packed dark brown sugar

$\frac{1}{4}$ cup peanut oil

$\frac{1}{2}$ teaspoon garlic powder

1 tablespoon seasoned salt

$\frac{1}{2}$ teaspoon ground black pepper

1 teaspoon Louisiana hot sauce or 1 teaspoon
   cayenne pepper (optional)

3 to 4 drops red food coloring (optional)

In a medium saucepan over high heat, combine all the ingredients and bring to a boil. Immediately reduce the heat to low and simmer, uncovered, for 20 minutes. Use this sauce to baste beef or poultry in the last 15 minutes of grilling. If you're using the sauce to cover chicken wings, add hot sauce or the cayenne.

For a dramatic effect, you can add the red food coloring at the last moment, stir into the sauce, and enjoy the reactions of your guests.

Makes 4 to $4\frac{1}{2}$ cups

JAMAICAN JERK SAUCE

Recipe loaned to me by a woman at a jerk restaurant near Montego Bay, Jamaica. She wrote it down on the back of a brown paper bag, then put my take-away order in the bag and wished me "Good eatin', Mon!" She did not give specific amounts of the various spices: "I do it by what feels good," she related, "so just makes up yo' own." Have a fire extinguisher ready . . . this is hot stuff!

$\frac{1}{2}$ cup allspice berries

$\frac{1}{2}$ cup packed brown sugar

6 to 8 garlic cloves

4 to 6 Scotch bonnet peppers (see Note)

1 tablespoon dried thyme

1 to 2 bunches green onions

1 teaspoon cinnamon

$\frac{1}{2}$ teaspoon nutmeg

Salt and pepper to taste

4 tablespoons soy sauce

210

Put all the ingredients in a food processor or blender and liquefy. Pour the sauce into a glass jar or plastic container, cover, and keep refrigerated. Do not store in a metal container, as the peppers can eat into the metal and cause contamination. The sauce will keep forever if refrigerated properly.

Use it on chicken, lamb, pork, beef, venison, rabbit or, you guessed it, anything you cook that in any way resembles meat or poultry. This sauce would be overwhelming for most fish dishes, though.

Note: Please, please be very careful when handling Scotch bonnet peppers (the hottest peppers on the planet). Use rubber or plastic gloves whenever you handle peppers, and if these are not available, wash your hands *thoroughly* after handling. One mistaken rubbing of an eye and you will never forget the experience!

Makes 1 $\frac{1}{2}$ cups

A mop is the *only* way to sauce eight hundred pounds of pork shoulder in Owensboro.

JACK'S WHISKEY BBQ SAUCE

Adapted from a recipe seen at the Jack Daniel's World Invitational Barbecue Contest in Lynchburg, Tennessee.

$\frac{1}{2}$ pint Jack Daniel's whiskey

1 can tomato soup

1 tablespoon Worcestershire sauce

Pinch of garlic powder

2 tablespoons brown sugar

1 teaspoon ground white pepper

Dash of Louisiana hot sauce

Mix all the ingredients in a medium saucepan over medium heat, stirring constantly for 5 minutes. Remove from the heat and pour into a medium bowl to cool. When cooled, put in a sealable glass or plastic bottle.

Use this sauce on anything you barbecue, but it's especially good on grilled leg of lamb and grilled lamb riblets.

Makes 2 to 2$\frac{1}{2}$ cups

KEY WEST CITRUS SAUCE

This is wonderful on just about any grilled or smoked fish and equally as tasty on BBQ chicken or other poultry.

3 cups ketchup

2 cups tightly packed dark brown sugar

1 tablespoon dry mustard

$\frac{1}{2}$ cup lime juice

$\frac{1}{2}$ cup onion juice

$\frac{3}{4}$ cup mango juice

$\frac{3}{4}$ cup orange juice

$\frac{3}{4}$ cup pineapple juice

1 tablespoon black pepper

Pinch of salt

Pinch of cumin

4 to 5 tablespoons cornstarch

Combine all the ingredients except the cornstarch in a large glass or ceramic bowl, mixing well with a spoon until fully blended. Pour the sauce into a large glass or ceramic pot, add 2 tablespoons of the cornstarch, and cook over low heat until the mixture thickens, about 5 minutes. If the sauce is still too thin, slowly add more cornstarch, 1 tablespoon at a time, stirring, until you reach the desired thickness. Take the sauce off the heat and cool it, uncovered. When the sauce is cool, pour it into sealable jars or plastic containers. Can be used as a marinade or basting sauce, or warmed and served at the table with the entree.

Makes 9 to 10 cups

213

KIWI BEER MARINADE

Marcus Knight, Auckland, New Zealand

The "Kiwi" refers to the origin of the recipe, as New Zealanders like to be called Kiwis after their national bird. No kiwi fruit is used in this recipe.

1 can beer

1 small can tomato soup

1 tablespoon sweet chili sauce

2 tablespoons soy sauce

1 tablespoon Worcestershire sauce

3 garlic cloves, crushed

1 teaspoon brown sugar

$\frac{1}{2}$ teaspoon dried savory

$\frac{1}{2}$ teaspoon dried oregano

$\frac{1}{2}$ teaspoon dried basil

Dash of red wine

$\frac{1}{2}$ teaspoon sea salt

$\frac{1}{2}$ teaspoon lemon or citrus pepper

Mix all the ingredients in a medium glass or metal bowl. Put any meat or poultry you wish to marinate in a Ziploc bag and add the marinade, seal the bag, and refrigerate overnight.

Drain the meat or poultry and cook it on your favorite barbecue. Enjoy the finished results with a cold New Zealand Steinlager beer.

Makes 2 to 2$\frac{1}{2}$ cups

214

KOREAN BULGOGI MARINADE

Recipe learned by watching a cook in the kitchen of the Grand Hyatt Hotel on lovely, tropical Cheju Do Island in Korea.

1 cup soy sauce

1 cup brown sugar

3 to 4 garlic cloves, minced

1 inch ginger root, peeled and minced

2 tablespoons sesame oil

1 bunch green onions, finely chopped

In a small saucepan over low heat, combine the soy sauce, brown sugar, garlic, and ginger, and stir until the sugar is dissolved. Remove from the heat and add the remaining ingredients.

This is a super marinade or basting sauce for Tri-tip, beef for sandwiches, and beef ribs. You can use it as a marinade, baste, or serving sauce. But since there is sugar in this sauce you can only use it to baste during the last 5 minutes that the meat is on the barbecue or the sugar will burn.

Makes 2 cups

From lemons and limes to mustard and honey, grillers across the nation get creative when making their own barbecue sauces!

LAST GAUCHO BEEFSTEAK SAUCE

Claus Meyer, Rio de Janeiro, Brazil

In Argentina and Brazil, this sauce is served beside juicy grilled steaks.

1 cup chopped Italian parsley

$\frac{1}{2}$ cup olive oil

$\frac{1}{4}$ cup red wine vinegar

1 tablespoon chopped garlic

1 teaspoon dried oregano

1 teaspoon red pepper flakes

$\frac{1}{2}$ teaspoon coarse salt

1 teaspoon chopped fresh thyme (optional)

1 tablespoon chopped fresh rosemary (optional)

218

In a medium bowl, mix the ingredients well and let them marinate in the refrigerator for at least a day. You may add thyme and rosemary if you like, but in very small amounts. Remove the mixture from the refrigerator. In a medium saucepan over high heat, boil the liquid for 10 minutes. Serve the steak sauce in a sauceboat alongside medium-rare steaks.

Makes $1\frac{3}{4}$ cups

GAIL'S GUAVA BBQ SAUCE

Gail Miller, Nome, Alaska

10 ounces guava jelly

2 teaspoons dry mustard

$\frac{1}{4}$ cup lemon juice

4 tablespoons white vinegar

1 teaspoon ground cumin

2 shallots, minced

2 green onions, green part only, minced

$\frac{1}{4}$ cup dry sherry

3 tablespoons tomato paste

2 tablespoons brown sugar

1 lemon, thinly sliced

Combine all the ingredients in a medium saucepan, stir, and bring to a boil over medium heat. Immediately reduce the heat to low and simmer for 30 minutes. Remove the sauce from the heat and cool.

With a brush, baste pork ribs or fish (salmon and halibut work especially well) several times during the last 10 minutes of cooking only. Serve extra sauce on the side with freshly sliced lemons floating on the surface.

Makes 1 to 1$\frac{1}{2}$ cups

LEXINGTON "YALLER" SAUCE

This is near to being the *only* kind of sauce served in some parts of North Carolina. Incredible on a pulled pork shoulder sandwich, served on hamburger buns. Add a little of the mustard-based coleslaw and you're in hog heaven, North Carolina style.

$\frac{3}{4}$ cup yellow mustard

$\frac{3}{4}$ cup red wine vinegar

$\frac{1}{2}$ teaspoon Worcestershire sauce

2 tablespoon butter

1$\frac{1}{2}$ teaspoons salt

$\frac{1}{4}$ cup brown sugar

1 teaspoon ground black pepper

$\frac{1}{2}$ teaspoon Louisiana hot sauce

In a medium saucepan, combine the ingredients, stirring to blend. Over low heat, simmer 30 minutes, stirring until thoroughly blended. Let stand at room temperature for 1 hour before using.

Makes 2 cups

MONGO'S MANGO MARINADE

2 whole limes
2 tablespoons lime juice
1 cup mango chutney
1 teaspoon brown sugar
$\frac{1}{4}$ cup light corn syrup
Pinch of marjoram
$\frac{1}{8}$ teaspoon red pepper

220

Peel the limes, saving the zest from one of them and chopping it finely. Cut the limes in half, deseed them, and put them in a food processor. Add the lime juice, lime zest, chutney, and brown sugar. Pulse until the lime is fairly well chopped up, although it will still be chunky.

Pour this mixture into a bowl and add the corn syrup, marjoram, and red pepper, and mix well.

Pour the mixture into sealable glass or plastic containers and refrigerate until ready to use as a marinade, baste, or serving sauce. Absolutely superb on halibut, shark, and salmon.

Makes 1 to $1\frac{1}{2}$ cups

MOMMA'S MARVELOUS MARGARITA GLAZE

Barbara Smith, Southington, Connecticut

Barbara learned this from her big sister, Kathy, under supervision of their father, Dennis.

$\frac{1}{2}$ cup Triple Sec
$\frac{1}{2}$ cup lime juice
$\frac{1}{2}$ cup tequila
$\frac{1}{2}$ cup honey
Pinch of salt

Mix all the ingredients in a medium saucepan over low heat, stirring constantly for 4 to 5 minutes. When the glaze is thoroughly mixed, remove from the heat and cool. When cooled you can bottle it or use the glaze straight from the pan to brush over chicken, fish, or shellfish.

Try basting shrimp with this or use it as a dip for cooked chicken wings or shrimp. Or you can drizzle the glaze on grilled oysters or clams, after the shells have opened.

221

Makes 2 cups

REMUS'S KANSAS CITY CLASSIC SAUCE

Remus Powers, Kansas City, Missouri

Remus is the originator of the Diddy-Wa-Diddy Sauce Contest, held during the American Royal Barbecue Contest.

$\frac{1}{4}$ teaspoon ground allspice

$\frac{1}{4}$ teaspoon ground cinnamon

$\frac{1}{4}$ teaspoon ground mace

$\frac{1}{4}$ teaspoon black pepper

$\frac{1}{2}$ teaspoon curry powder, Oriental preferred

$\frac{1}{2}$ teaspoon chili powder

$\frac{1}{2}$ teaspoon paprika

$\frac{1}{4}$ cup white vinegar

$\frac{1}{2}$ teaspoon hot pepper sauce

1 cup ketchup

$\frac{1}{3}$ cup dark molasses

Place all of the dry ingredients into a bowl. Add the vinegar and stir. Add the hot pepper sauce, ketchup, and molasses, and stir until the mixture is thoroughly blended. This sauce may be served at room temperature or heated.

Adds a wonderful zip and burst of flavor to beef brisket, pork tenderloin, and lamb chops.

Makes 1$\frac{1}{2}$ cups

The heart and soul of Arthur Bryant's in Kansas City: trays full of hot-from-the-pit beef brisket and pork shoulder.

VIDALIA BAR-BE-CUE SAUCE

1 large Vidalia onion (see Notes), finely chopped

1 cup cider vinegar

$\frac{1}{2}$ cup cider

$\frac{1}{4}$ cup lemon juice

$\frac{1}{3}$ cup distilled (white) vinegar

5 tablespoons prepared yellow mustard

3 teaspoons A-1 sauce

4 tablespoons honey

2 teaspoons brown sugar

3 cups ketchup

1 teaspoon mesquite seasoning salt (see Notes)

1 teaspoon black pepper

$\frac{1}{4}$ pound butter or margarine

224

In a medium saucepan, mix all the ingredients together well, and simmer for 10 to 15 minutes, stirring often. This sauce works especially well with beef, but can be used for just about any barbecue meat, poultry, or fish.

Notes: Depending on where you live, you can substitute Walla Walla or Maui onions, or any variety deemed "sweet." If sweet onions are unavailable, increase the honey by 2 teaspoons.

Mesquite seasoning salt is available on-line from Oregon Spice Company (www.oregonspice.com).

Makes 5 cups

TYBET'S SOUTHERN COLA BARBEQUE SAUCE

Tyler and Betsy Smith, Southington, Connecticut

One 12-ounce can cola (see Note)

$1\frac{1}{2}$ cups ketchup

1 cup finely chopped onion

$\frac{1}{4}$ cup cider vinegar

2 tablespoons A-1 steak sauce

1 teaspoon Mexene chili powder

2 teaspoon lemon granules

1 teaspoon sugar

1 teaspoon salt

White pepper to taste

In a medium saucepan over high heat, combine all the ingredients and bring to a boil, stirring often. Immediately reduce the heat to low and simmer, covered, stirring occasionally, for 30 to 45 minutes, or until the sauce is thickened. Remove the pan from the heat, let the mixture cool, and then store in a tightly covered glass jar or plastic container.

Note: Do *not* use diet sodas. They turn bitter when cooked.

Makes $4\frac{1}{2}$ to 5 cups

225

RUB A DUB DUB, BUB!

The following are quick rubs to delight the culinary senses. They taste good, too! and are easy to make and use. The ingredients should be mixed together well, rubbed gently into meat, fish, poultry, or game with your hands and left to dry-marinate for at least 4 hours, but preferably overnight. Then it's time to grill, smoke, or charbroil to your heart's content.

BOB TAIL RUB

3 tablespoons mild paprika

2 teaspoons seasoned salt

2 teaspoons freshly ground black pepper

2 teaspoons garlic powder

1 teaspoon cayenne pepper, not too hot

1 teaspoon dried summer savory

1 teaspoon dry mustard

$\frac{1}{2}$ teaspoon chili powder

1 teaspoon ground thyme

1 teaspoon ground coriander

2 teaspoons green peppercorns

1 teaspoon ground allspice

BRANDY'S RUBBING POWDER

1 teaspoon garlic powder

1 tablespoon honey granules

1 teaspoon green onion powder

$\frac{1}{2}$ teaspoon ground thyme

1 tablespoon lemon granules

1 tablespoon Worcestershire powder (see Note)

1 teaspoon sugar

Note: Available on-line from Oregon Spice Company (www.oregonspice.com).

CURRIED RUB

$\frac{1}{4}$ cup chili powder

1 teaspoon onion powder

1 teaspoon curry powder

1 teaspoon ground cumin

1 teaspoon garlic powder

1 teaspoon dry mustard

1 teaspoon white pepper

1 teaspoon dried oregano

2 teaspoons celery salt

1 teaspoon dried parsley flakes

RED RIVER RUB

1 teaspoon cayenne pepper

1 teaspoon curry powder

1 teaspoon turmeric

1 teaspoon ground ginger

1 teaspoon ground cumin

1 tablespoon Mexene chili powder

1 tablespoon paprika

Dash of nutmeg

LAST ROUNDUP BEEF RUB

Caleb Pirtle III, Dallas, Texas

$\frac{1}{2}$ teaspoon lemon pepper

$\frac{1}{4}$ teaspoon ground rosemary

4 teaspoons garlic powder

4 teaspoons onion powder

1 tablespoon Worcestershire powder (see Note)

1 teaspoon paprika

1 teaspoon beef bouillon granules

2 teaspoons Montreal steak seasoning

2 teaspoons salt

2 tablespoons coarsely ground black pepper

Combine all the ingredients in a large bowl, mixing well. Use immediately or store tightly sealed in glass or plastic container. Shake before each use to remix the spices.

228

Note: Available on-line from Oregon Spice Company (www.oregonspice.com).

Makes 8 ounces

BAXTER BB CHICKEN'S BACK (AND EVERYWHERE ELSE, TOO) RUB

Marsha and Russ Matta, from somewhere on their sailboat, somewhere on the Columbia River

1 tablespoon garlic powder

1 tablespoon green onion powder

1 tablespoon honey granules

1 teaspoon white pepper

1 tablespoon mild curry powder

1 tablespoon brown sugar

1 tablespoon soy sauce powder (see Note)

1 teaspoon Montreal chicken seasoning

In a small bowl, mix all the ingredients well with a spoon. Pour into a glass jar that has a shaker top and use to sprinkle on barbecued or roast chicken. Keep in a cool, dry place so spices don't form a useless cake.

Note: Available on-line from Oregon Spice Company (www.oregonspice.com).

Makes 8 ounces

THREE IDDIE FISHIES RUB

Anne and Terry Callon, Jalisco, Mexico

1 tablespoon onion powder

1 tablespoon sugar

1 tablespoon dried summer savory

1 teaspoon McCormick's imitation butter flavor salt

1 teaspoon green tea leaves

1 teaspoon finely ground black pepper

1 tablespoon lemon granules

1 tablespoon ground ginger

In a small bowl, mix all the ingredients well with a spoon. Pour into a glass jar with a shaker top and use to sprinkle on barbecued, broiled, or panfried fish. Keep in a cool, dry place so spices don't form a useless cake.

Makes 8 ounces

★ NAME DE LA FLAME ★
Barbecue Team Names We Love

Adribbers
A Hobby Gone Awry
Airpork Crew
Always Rubbin' Somethin'
Any Pork in a Storm
Aporkalypse Now
Armed & Hammered
Artrageous Cookers
Asleep at the Grill
Badges, Brews & BBQ's
Bama Butt Burners
Barbeque Republic
Barefoot in the Pork
Barn Burners
Basty Boys
Baxter's Beer-Butt Cookin' Team
Becky & the Blind Puppy
Beefy Cowboys
Beer, Meat, and Rebar
Beer Nutz
Beverly Pigbillies
Big Bad Wolf & 3 Little Pigs
Big Bee Que
Big Momma & Uncle Fats
Bite My Butt
Blazin' Bacon
Blood, Sweat, & Que
Boars 'R' US

Bob-a-Que
Bovine & Swine BBQ
Brisket Cases
Brunt Ends
Bubbaque Boys
Buck & Wing Cooking Team
Bucken-Far-B-Que
Bum Steers
Buns & Roses
Burning Desires
Burning Sensation
Burnt Offerings
Butt Naked Barbecue
Byte My Ribs
C Mor Butts
Can't Quit Smokin'
Car Dogs BBQ
Cayenne Social Club
Char Czar
Chicken Chokin' Smokin'
Cochran Juris Porkers
Cowboy Yacht Club
Crispy Critters
Damnifino
Dead Meat BBQ
Denver Dine-O-Might
Dirty Dick & the Legless
   Wonders

Dizzy Pig BBQ
Don't Burn the Beer
Dr. Frankenswine
Dr. I Can't Stop Smoking
Drag N' Smoke
Dueling Bubbas
Dyin' to Smoke
Exhausted Rooster Club
Fat Chance BBQ
Fat, Drunk, & Stupid
First Pig & Loining Bank
Gar B Que
Gas Hawgs
Genuswine
Gettin' Piggy with It
Girth Wind and Fire
Got Pig?
Grand Masters of Cooking
   Disasters
Great Grill O Fire
Green Eggs & Hog
Grillas
Grilligan's Island
Grillin' 'N' Chillin'
Half Fast Cookers
Ham Hocks 'N' Dirty Socks
Harrah's Porker Chips
Heartburn BBQ

Heavenly Piglets	Junk Yard Hogs	Oink, Inc.
Hidin' from Our Wives	Kill It, Chill It, Grill It	Operation Rolling Smoke
Highway Ribbery	Let's Kick Some Ash	Orthopigs
Hocus Smokus	Mac Daddy Meat	Oscar & The Grouches
Hogaholics	Macon Bacon Cookers	Outhouse BBQ
Hogapalooza	Master Basters	Pepper Mike & the Fire-breathers
Hogasm	Me and My Pig	
Hoggie & the Blowpigs	Meateorites	Peyton Place Motley Crew
Hog Rock Cafe	Meatloafers	P.H.A.T. Chance
Hog Tied	Meat Me In KC	Piggin' N Grinnin'
Hogwizer	Mis-B-Havin'	Pig Newtons
Holy Cow Cookers	Modern Porkfolio Theory	Pig'n & Swig'n
Hook & Crooks	Moon Swiners	Piggy Licious
Inlaws & Outlaws	Moose & Lobster Preserva-tion Society	Pig Pounda Kappa
In Porcus Veritas		Pigs-R-Us
Iowa Hawgeyes	Natural Born Grillers	Pirates of the Car-Rib-Bean
I Smell Smoke	Not Ready for Swine Time Porkers	Pits & Ashes
Jacques Strappe & Supporters		Poke in da Eye
Jamakin Ba Ba Q	Nude BBQ	Pok N' da Ribs
Joint Chiefs of Smoke	Oink, Cackle, & Moo	Pork Authority

This Austrian team traveled to Lynchburg, Tennessee, to compete in the Jack Daniel's Invitational and made author Rick Browne an honorary member.

Porkbarrel Legislators
Porkcrastinators
Porkey & Beans
Pork Floyd BBQ Team
Porkin' Ain't Easy
Porkitects
Pork Me Tender
Porkosaurus
Porkstruction
Porn 'N' Bones
Portfolio of Pork
Pot Bellied Cookers
Prime Swine International
Pyropigmaniacs
Que 'N' Brew
Ribs, for Her Pleasure
Rib Ticklers
Roadkill BBQ Company
Shut Up & Cook

Smokelicious
Smokin' Bovine
Smok'n in the Boys Room
Sow Luau
Sweet Swine O' Mine
Swine & Dine
Swinefeld
Swine Flew
Swine Tingling BBQ
Swiney Ribbers
Team Stupid
Ten That Grilled Elvis
The Grate Pretenders
The Hogfather
The Meat Loafers
The Missing Links
The Pit & the Pigulum
The Sowpranos
The Sprice Grills

Three Brisketeers
Three Carps & a Tarp
3 Fat Guys & a Smoker
3rd Degree Burn
TNT BBQ Co.
Tom & John's Orgasmic Slabs
Top Gun Brisketeers
Totally Boar'd
Transporkers
Turn & Burn
Tush Hawgs
Two Jokers with a Smoker
We "Auto" Be Grillin'
We B Q' N
We B Smokin'
Westport Weinies
Whole Hog Café
You Choke It We Smoke It

ATTLEMEN'S

Date May 19, 2001

Pay to the order of _Viking Cooking Team_ $ 750.00

Seven Hundred Fifty and 00/100 Dollars

BARBECUE
COOKING CONTEST

Memo _Anything But - Beef_   Reckitt Benckiser

1st Place

2001 MIM BBQ

VEGETARIAN BBQ

GOLDEN ROSEMARY POLENTA

One 24-ounce log prepared polenta
2 teaspoons extra virgin olive oil
Garlic salt to taste
Lemon pepper to taste
2 tablespoons chopped fresh rosemary leaves

Prepare a hot charcoal fire or preheat the gas grill to high.

Cut the polenta into twelve $\frac{1}{2}$-inch-thick slices. Place the slices on a baking sheet. Brush both sides of the polenta rounds with olive oil and season lightly with the garlic salt and lemon pepper, and sprinkle with the rosemary. Lightly oil the grill rack and cook the polenta slices over high heat (500° to 600°F) until nicely browned, 3 to 5 minutes per side. Serve on a heated platter.

Serves 4 to 6

236

FANTASIA'S BBQ TOFU CAKES

Fantasia, Maui, Hawaii

An earth mother and blithe spirit who bubbles love for mother earth, and every living thing on the face of the planet.

1 tablespoon arrowroot powder

$\frac{1}{4}$ cup barley miso

$\frac{1}{2}$ cup mirin

$\frac{1}{4}$ cup plum sauce

1 tablespoon brown sugar

2 tablespoons honey

12 small Japanese eggplants,
   or American variety

1 bunch green onions

8 whole, fresh shiitake mushrooms

4 atsu-age cakes (firm, thick, deep-fried tofu),
   available at health food stores

237

In a small saucepan, over medium heat on a grill or the stovetop, whisk together the arrowroot and $\frac{1}{2}$ cup of water. Cook for 2 to 3 minutes, stirring constantly, and add miso, mirin, plum sauce, brown sugar, and honey, and cook for 5 minutes until thickened. Remove from the heat, pour into a medium bowl, and let cool. Reserve.

Slice each eggplant in half lengthwise (if using the American variety slice in $\frac{1}{2}$-inch-thick rounds) and trim the ends from the green onions. Clean the shiitake mushrooms.

Brush the grill with sesame oil to prevent sticking. Cook the atsu-age tofu cakes over medium-hot coals (450° to 550°F) 7 to 8 minutes each side until the edges start to crisp and turn brown. While the tofu grills, place the whole green onions, mushrooms, and eggplants (cut side down) on the grill and cook for 5 minutes. Turn and baste with the miso-plum sauce. Continue cooking for 5 to 8 minutes until eggplants can be pierced easily with a fork.

Serve the tofu cakes with the grilled vegetables on top and drizzle both with the remaining miso-plum sauce.

Serves 4 to 6

Goode Co.
BARBEQUE
"You might give
some serious though[t]
to thanking your
lucky stars you're
in Texas".

SCOTT BAR B QUE
BAR BQ PORK $800 LB

ALL
SANDWICHES   REGULAR 225
                  JUMBO $275
SLAW   HOMEMADE
&
BEANS   HALF PINT 100
         PINT   225
         QUART   450

BUNS
        ALL   12 $ 145   BAR-B-QUE
        REGULAR &   TAX INCLUDED
        PACK   8 $ 115   IN PRICES

GRILLED LEMON-LIME TEMPEH

MARINADE

2 tablespoons freshly squeezed lime juice

$\frac{1}{4}$ cup freshly squeezed lemon juice

$\frac{1}{4}$ cup olive oil

$\frac{1}{4}$ teaspoon dried summer savory

$\frac{1}{4}$ teaspoon dried thyme

1 tablespoon raspberry leaves (see Note)

$\frac{1}{8}$ teaspoon black pepper

16 ounces tempeh

1 large sweet onion, sliced

Fresh lettuce leaves for garnish

Sliced tomatoes for garnish

4 to 6 hamburger rolls (whole wheat)

240

Heat the grill to high, about 400°F.

In a small bowl, combine the marinade ingredients, mix well, and set aside. Cut the tempeh into 1-inch strips and place in a metal or bamboo steamer or over boiling water. Steam for 15 to 18 minutes until heated through. Remove and drain the tempeh, then place it in a 2- to 4-quart flat casserole dish or Pyrex baking dish. Pour the marinade over the tempeh, add the onions, and marinate in the refrigerator for 4 to 6 hours.

Grill the tempeh and onions over a medium-hot (400° to 500°F) BBQ grill you've sprayed or coated with oil, basting the tempeh frequently with the marinade. Grill each side until it's heated through and appears a light brown.

Serve the tempeh slices and onions on the hamburger rolls. Garnish with onion slices, lettuce, and sliced tomatoes. Have your favorite BBQ sauce ready on the side for those who wish to add it to their grilled sandwiches.

Note: Raspberry leaves are available on-line through the Oregon Spice Company (www.oregonspice.com).

Serves 4 to 6

TOFU STEAKS WITH PINEAPPLE-MANGO SALSA

1 bunch fresh cilantro

$\frac{2}{3}$ cup vegetable stock

$\frac{1}{4}$ cup lemon juice

1 tablespoon crushed red pepper

$\frac{1}{4}$ cup minced fresh ginger

1 tablespoon brown sugar

1 teaspoon blackstrap molasses

5 garlic cloves

Black pepper to taste

$1\frac{1}{4}$ pounds firm tofu, drained, cut lengthwise into four
    1-inch-thick "steaks"

1 small fresh pineapple

2 mangoes

241

Chop the cilantro to make $\frac{1}{2}$ cup and set aside 1 tablespoon for the salsa. In a medium baking dish, combine the chopped cilantro and the stock, lemon juice, red pepper, ginger, brown sugar, molasses, garlic, and black pepper. Stir and add the tofu. Marinate it for 2 hours at room temperature.

Peel the pineapple and mangoes, then finely chop, discarding the pineapple skin and core and the mango skin and pit. In a medium serving bowl, combine the fruit and 1 tablespoon of the reserved chopped cilantro. Set it aside at room temperature to let the flavors combine.

Prepare an outdoor grill for medium heat. Drain the tofu, reserving the marinade. Lightly oil the grill and place the tofu on it. Grill the tofu until lightly browned, 4 to 5 minutes, brushing frequently with the marinade and turning once. Serve the tofu steaks with the pineapple and mango mixture.

Serves 4

RICK'S GRILLED RATTA-TOOEY

1 medium eggplant, about 1 pound

2 medium onions (Walla Walla, Vidalia,
   or Maui preferred)

1 medium summer squash or zucchini

1 large golden or red bell pepper

1 large, ripe tomato, seeded and diced

$\frac{1}{4}$ cup chopped black olives

2 tablespoons chopped fresh basil

2 tablespoons chopped fresh cilantro

1 teaspoon fines herbes

1 teaspoon dried oregano

2 tablespoons red wine vinegar

2 tablespoons olive oil

Sea or coarse salt to taste

Freshly ground black pepper to taste

$\frac{1}{4}$ pound asiago cheese (optional)

Cut the eggplant into $\frac{1}{2}$-inch-thick slices. Salt them on both sides and place them in a colander for 30 minutes, then rinse and drain. You may cut off the peel if you wish.

Peel the onions and cut them in $\frac{1}{2}$-inch slices. Quarter the summer squash or zucchini lengthwise. Cut the bell pepper into $\frac{1}{2}$-inch pieces lengthwise.

Prepare a hot grill (500° to 600°F). Brush the vegetables lightly with olive oil. Grill the eggplant on both sides until nicely browned and quite tender, 12 to 15 minutes total. Grill the onions, bell pepper, and summer squash or zucchini on both sides until tender and marked with brown, about 10 minutes total. (You may want to use a vegetable basket or grid to prevent the veggies from sliding into the fire.) Remove the veggies from the grill, place in a medium bowl, and let them cool.

When all the vegetables are cool enough to handle, chop them into fairly large chunks and combine them in a serving bowl.

Stir in the tomato, olives, basil, cilantro, fines herbes, oregano, vinegar, and the 2 tablespoons olive oil, and toss well. Season with salt and pepper. If desired, sprinkle the top with crumbled asiago cheese. Serve at room temperature with grilled garlic bread or foccacia.

Serves 4 to 6

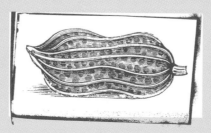

OLE OLE INFREE'S TEMPEH SATAY

Dave Olson, Vancouver, Washington, and Paheo, Hawaii

Dave is one of the earth's most special people. A gentle man who truly is himself and who opened my eyes about lots of things including some incredible vegetarian recipes, such as this one.

MARINADE

$\frac{1}{2}$ cup grated coconut

$\frac{1}{4}$ cup orange juice

1 tablespoon honey

$\frac{1}{4}$ cup tamari (whole-wheat soy sauce)

$\frac{1}{8}$ teaspoon cayenne pepper

4 tempeh cutlets

243

PEANUT SAUCE

$\frac{1}{4}$ cup smooth peanut butter

$\frac{1}{4}$ cup finely chopped roasted peanuts

3 tablespoons tamari

1 tablespoon mirin or sherry

$\frac{1}{2}$ teaspoon rice vinegar

$\frac{1}{8}$ teaspoon garlic powder

1 tablespoon honey

1 cup nonfat yogurt, plain

$\frac{1}{8}$ teaspoon cayenne pepper

One 16-ounce can pineapple chunks

To make the marinade, puree $\frac{1}{4}$ cup of the coconut with the orange juice, honey, tamari, and cayenne in a blender until smooth, 2 to 3 minutes. Pour the marinade into a shallow baking dish. Cut the tempeh into 1-inch cubes and add it to the marinade. Set aside for 30 minutes.

In a small saucepan, blend together the peanut sauce ingredients with a wire whisk, and warm the sauce on low heat for 7 to 8 minutes. Do not let it boil.

Thread the tempeh cubes and pineapple chunks onto bamboo skewers that have been soaked in hot water for 20 minutes.

Grill the tempeh-pineapple skewers on a grill over medium-hot coals, 3 to 5 minutes on each side, or until cubes start to get brown edges. Brush the kebabs with the marinade two to three times during cooking. When the kebabs are browned on all sides they are done. Remove from the heat and set on a platter. Sprinkle with the remaining coconut.

Serve immediately with warm peanut sauce.

Serves 4

244

DAVE'S SEITAN GRILLING SAUCE

1½ cups thick tomato sauce

3 tablespoons honey

1 tablespoon molasses

1 tablespoon olive oil

2 tablespoons soy sauce

1 tablespoon paprika

1 tablespoon chili powder

1 tablespoon mustard

1 teaspoon garlic powder

1 teaspoon dried oregano

Combine all the ingredients in a large bowl and mix well. Cover and let the mixture stand for at least 1 hour before using. Refrigerate in a tightly sealed bottle if not using right away. Use as a marinade for grilled tofu, seitan, or tempeh.

Makes 1½ cups

BBQED SEITAN BURGERS

As a nonvegetarian I was shocked at how good these are. They take a while to make, but the flavors are wonderful and they're as healthy as you can get. Garnish these with tomato, avocado, red onion, or dill pickle slices.

12 ounces seitan

1 tablespoon olive oil

4 medium shallots, minced

$\frac{1}{2}$ pound button mushrooms, chopped

1 large portobello mushroom, chopped

1 teaspoon sea salt

1 teaspoon dried chives

1 teaspoon dried summer savory

1 teaspoon ground ginger

$\frac{1}{8}$ teaspoon red pepper flakes

$\frac{1}{2}$ cup whole-wheat bread flour

$\frac{1}{2}$ cup yellow cornmeal

2 teaspoons Mexene chili powder

$\frac{1}{2}$ teaspoon granulated garlic

1 teaspoon ground cumin

$\frac{1}{4}$ teaspoon black pepper

$\frac{1}{4}$ cup favorite BBQ sauce

$\frac{1}{4}$ cup dark cane syrup

1 tablespoon concentrated lime juice

6 to 8 wheat hamburger buns or focaccia

Drain the seitan, squeezing to remove excess liquid, then roughly chop. This amount should make 2 cups. Process the seitan in a food blender until it resembles a large-grind hamburger, which should be accomplished in several short pulses.

In a cast-iron skillet, heat the olive oil over medium heat. Add the shallots and cook, stirring often, until softened, or 3 to 4 minutes. Add the chopped button and portobello mushrooms, $\frac{1}{2}$ teaspoon of the salt, chives, savory, ginger, and red pepper flakes, and cook for 4 to 5 minutes, stirring often, until heated through and well mixed. Transfer the ingredients to a large bowl and let the mixture cool. Add the ground seitan and mix well with your hands or with a wooden spoon.

In a large bowl, mix together the flour, cornmeal, chili powder, granulated garlic, cumin, remaining $\frac{1}{2}$ teaspoon salt, and pepper. Slowly stir the flour mixture into the seitan mixture until well combined. Using $\frac{1}{2}$ cup each, form the mixture into round and firm patties; you'll get 6 to 8. In a small bowl, mix the BBQ sauce, cane syrup, and lime juice, and set aside.

Place the seitan patties on a preoiled grill over medium-high heat (450° to 550°F), brushing liberally and often with the BBQ-cane syrup-lime sauce. Cook for 5 to 6 minutes, turn once, brush the other side with sauce, then cook another 4 to 5 minutes.

Separate the hamburger buns, brush them (or the foccacia) with olive oil, and grill for 1 to 2 minutes to brown the buns.

Present the seitan patties on the grilled buns with the remaining sauce on the side.

247

Serves 6 to 8

SMOKIN' TOFU'ED BBQ BEANS

$3\frac{1}{2}$ cups cooked Great Northern
   or navy beans
$1\frac{1}{2}$ cups cooked soybeans
1 cup chopped sweet onion
1 cup chopped bell pepper, yellow or red
2 garlic cloves, minced
One 8-ounce can tomato sauce
2 tablespoons molasses
3 tablespoons brown sugar
1 tablespoon cider vinegar
1 teaspoon prepared mustard
1 teaspoon ground ginger
$\frac{1}{4}$ teaspoon ground cinnamon
$\frac{1}{4}$ teaspoon ground allspice
$\frac{1}{4}$ teaspoon black pepper
1 teaspoon Beano (optional—to
   reduce the inherent gas in the beans)
2 tablespoons light molasses
2 tablespoons clover honey

248

Drain the Great Northern or navy beans and soybeans well. Combine them with all the remaining ingredients, except the molasses and honey, in a Dutch oven or flameproof cast-iron pot. Cover and bake the beans over indirect heat for $1\frac{1}{2}$ hours in a hot smoker or gas barbecue (325° to 350°F), or until the mixture is bubbling and the beans are just becoming soft. Remove the cover, stir the bean mixture, and cook for about 30 minutes longer.

    Mix the honey and molasses together and drizzle the mixture over the beans before serving

Serves 8

SMILLING
AND GROKING
Barbecue's Newest Cooking Style

More and more people are combining the techniques of grilling and smoking food in their backyard barbecues. The benefits of grilling include quicker cooking times and a charred ("barbecued") look to the meat, while smoking imparts a smoky flavor and moistness, albeit after a longer amount of time. Sometimes substantially longer. We are offering up a new style: **Smilling,** or, if you prefer, **Groking.**

Groking (or Smilling) is making use of the best characteristics of the two main styles of barbecue cooking.

We use the *quicker-heating* characteristics of grilling. Putting food over direct heat cooks it much quicker than either over indirect heat or in a smoker, where the food is mainly heated by the hot smoke from an adjacent firebox. The food cooks quicker and has a more "barbecued" look to it because of the grill marks caused by the very hot grill surface coming in contact with the food.

And we use the *flavor-producing* characteristics of smoking. Foods smoked over fragrant fruit and hardwoods have a super, well, "smoke" taste that enhances just about anything you place on a BBQ, and they are often more moist than grilled foods because the lower and slower cooking temperatures allow the natural juices to stay deep inside the food, instead of coming to the surface as often happens in grilling. That's why, when grilling, you should let the meat "rest" after it's cooked so the juices can go back inside the meat from the hot surface where they've been driven.

We've found the best way to combine the two heating/cooking methods is to begin on the grill. We can use either direct grilling, where the food is placed

right over the hot coals, briquettes, charcoal chunks, or gas flame, or the indirect heat method described on page 6.

Either does the trick, and both produce delicious, tender, and flavored meat, fish, and poultry.

For this chapter let's direct grill. And let's say we have a large roast to cook, perhaps a pork roast. First, you should prepare your smoke package. For this I like to take a large piece of heavy-duty aluminum foil (a square piece about 2 feet × 2 feet) and lay it flat on a table. Then take one or two handfuls of your favorite wood chips, pellets, or chunks of fruitwood, oak, hickory, pecan, maple, or mesquite, and mound the dry wood in the center of the sheet of foil.

Now, to be honest, there are two schools of thought on this process. Some insist that the wood needs to be soaked in water to produce more, better, or more consistent smoke. But others of us, including *moi,* think that wood has a more natural smoke if put in the packets dry. Unless you've poked holes all the way through the foil, the wood shouldn't catch fire. It will merely smolder along, sending clouds of yummy smoke up to and through the food you're cooking. So it's up to you: the wet method or the dry method, your choice.

Now fold one side over to the other on both sides, and the top and bottom, of the foil until you have a foil packet. Take a pencil or sharp knife and poke three to four small holes into the *top* of the foil only. Do not go entirely through the package. Now you have your smoke packet all ready.

Prepare the fire by heating the briquettes, coals, mesquite chunks, or gas flame until they are hot enough for your roast. When ready, and just before you put the grill over the coals or flame, place the smoke packet directly on the coals or a gas jet. Place the grill on top of the barbecue; place the meat, fish, or poultry on the grill; and close the lid.

Almost immediately the wood chunks in the foil begin to smolder and add their fragrant smoke to the food that's being grilled over the heat. Ta-da! you're Groking! Or is it Smilling? Whatever you want to call it, it's as easy as that.

When the pellets, chunks, or chips are all burned up, the smoke will stop. And a packet this size will provide plenty of flavorful smoke for just about any size roast, bird, or fish you want to cook on the grill. If you find you want more smoke, well, just repeat the packet preparation. Then lift the grill carefully, and add a new packet to the bed of coals or gas jets. You might want to reach in with a long pair of tongs and remove the old foil packet first, but that really isn't necessary.

Now we'll share some sage words of wisdom from one of the top experts in the field as to what woods to use in this process, and, of course, in normal grilling and smoking as well.

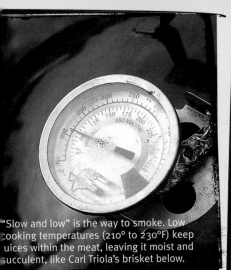

"Slow and low" is the way to smoke. Low cooking temperatures (210° to 230°F) keep juices within the meat, leaving it moist and succulent, like Carl Triola's brisket below.

WOODS TO USE IN GRILL-SMOKING

Dave DeWitt, editor, *Fiery Foods* magazine

This super article on how to, and how not to, use woods in grilling and smoking is reprinted with permission from *Fiery Foods* magazine. Check out the magazine or their website (www.fiery_foods.com) for great articles on both styles of barbecue cooking, recipes, and lots of information on cooking with hot peppers and chilis.

Two of the classic arts of grilling and barbecuing are knowing which woods to use and how to use them. Before I got a gas grill, all I had was a smoker, and I used the main chamber of it to grill meats over wood. It was by far the most challenging cooking I have ever done because the distance from the coals was fixed, and I had to estimate when the fire was the hottest so the meat would cook before the fire burned out. It is difficult to add wood during the grilling process because it takes so long for it to burn down to coals. Here are some hints:

The Tree with the Leguminous Smoke

You either love mesquite or hate it, depending on whether or not you're a farmer, hunter, cook, rancher, or woodworker. Farmers and ranchers hate the tree, of course, because it chokes out needed grazing grass, and, as a result of its extensive root system, is nearly impossible to remove from pastures.

A clump of mesquite trees provides shade, humidity, and food for such animals as doves, deer, javelina, and rabbits, which is why hunters like the tree. The mesquite beans, which are sugar-rich, provide food for both animals and man, and it once provided up to forty percent of the food in the diet of Native Americans in Texas. The wood of the tree is variously shaded, which is why woodworkers love it for making sculptures, gunstocks, parquet floors, and other hardwood products.

Cooks love mesquite because its wood produces a very hot flame, which is great for grilling steaks. Most mesquite trees these days are being cut down for wood chips and to make charcoal, but there's such an abundance of trees that there is no threat to mesquite.

Travelers all over the United States will have little trouble finding mesquite-grilled foods. But a hint to the home cook—the wood is used for grilling only because the smoke is considered to be too acrid for the lengthy smoking or barbecuing of meats. For that, pecan or hickory wood is suggested. And if you're grilling with mesquite, be sure to use aged wood because the green wood is too oily.

Other Woods

Do I really have to state in print not to use construction lumber scraps in your smoker or barbecue? Well, here I go. Most of these scraps are resinous pine or fir; some are treated or contain glue, like plywood. All are useless for cooking or smoking purposes. And, under no circumstances should you grill or smoke over woods such as cottonwood, willow, pine, or poplar. Stick to the woods listed below and you'll produce great heat and fragrant smoke. And when you consider smoking foods, think of the wood as a spice to add flavor instead of just being a fuel.

The woods that work best for grilling and smoking are hardwoods, particularly (for some unknown reason) the woods of certain fruit and nut trees. We should point out that any of these woods can be used to smoke any meat—we are just commenting on what meats these woods are commonly linked with. Some woods are available locally only where they grow, such as alder and pecan. But most woods are available by mail order or at your nearest barbecue supply store. In most cases, the hard remnants of fruits or nuts of the hardwood trees can also be used in the smoking process. Specifically, we mean peach pits and nut shells, but not acorns.

Alder imparts a light flavor that works well with fish and poultry. It is native to the northwestern United States, and is the traditional wood for smoking salmon.

Apple has a sweet, mild flavor and is used mostly with pork and game, but works with ham as well.

Cherry is also used for ham, but some cooks think that its smoke is too acrid.

Hickory is probably the most famous smoking hardwood. It's the wood of choice in the Southern barbecue belt. It imparts a strong, hearty flavor to meats, and is used mostly to smoke pork shoulders and ribs.

Maple is a mild and mellow smoke that imparts a sweet flavor that is traditional for smoking ham but is also good with poultry, pork, and seafood.

Oak, the favorite wood of Europe, is strong but not overpowering. A very

255

good wood for beef or lamb, it is probably the most versatile of the hardwoods. Do not use acorns for smoking.

Pecan is similar to hickory, but milder. It's also a Southern favorite that is becoming the smoking wood of choice in the Southwest because of the extensive pecan groves in Texas, New Mexico, and Arizona. Because of its availability, it is the wood most commonly used in our smoker.

Remember that the above woods can be mixed in the smoking process to add another dimension to barbecue. Some cooks in the Southwest, where I live, mix a little of the stronger mesquite in with pecan or applewood. Other woods used in the smoking process include **almond, black walnut, juniper** (slightly resinous), and **locust.**

More Smoke-Producing Plants

There are other woodlike flavorings to add to the heat source, but we don't recommend smoking with them for lengthy periods of time because they create smoke that is very intensely flavored. If you like the flavor of coconut, then smoke or grill fish with a little **coconut hull** added. Also, **grapevines** make a tart smoke that can overwhelm poultry or lamb. Use it sparingly. **Herbs,** such as **oregano, sage, thyme, marjoram, rosemary,** and **basil,** used both dried and fresh, can imbue the meat being smoked with their own particular flavor profiles. Since rosemary and sage have woody stems, their thick stems can be used as well as the branches and leaves. As with grapevine, a little herb—in either form—goes a long way.

Incidentally, do not burn chili pods to flavor grilled or smoked meat. The pods produce an acrid smoke—so irritating that Native Americans burned huge piles of them in an attempt to use gas warfare against the invading Conquistadors.

Some Final Hints

Match the wood to the meat.

If possible, use a thermometer to check the heat of your smoke when smoking meats, and make sure it is under 200°F.

Keep a squirt bottle next to the grill to instantly fight flare-ups.

Also, keep a long fork or tongs ready to remove the meat from the grill if flare-ups start. If possible, the meat should be removed as the water is being sprayed.

258

If using wood chips on charcoal or gas to flavor grilled foods, you may wish to soak them in water first.

Never use eucalyptus for grilling or smoking.

STOPPING BY SOME WOODS ON A SMOKY EVENING...

Other woods you can use:

Acacia: Same family as mesquite and has a similar flavor but not quite as heavy. Burns very hot.

Almond: A sweet smoke flavor, light ash. Good with most meats. Try it with shrimp or lobster.

Ash: Fast-burning wood that gives off a light, gentle, distinctive flavor. Good with fish and red meats.

Birch: Medium-hard wood with a flavor similar to maple. Good with pork and poultry, especially turkey.

Cottonwood: It is very subtle in flavor. Use with other woods like hickory, oak, pecan for more flavor. Don't use green cottonwood.

Crabapple: Similar to applewood. Baby back ribs take the flavor nicely.

Lilac: Very light, subtle with a hint of floral. Good with seafood and lamb.

Mulberry: The smell is sweet and reminds one of apple. Try it with brisket.

Orange, lemon, and grapefruit: Produce a mild smoky flavor. Excellent with beef, pork, fish, and poultry.

Pear: A nice subtle smoke flavor. Much like apple. Excellent with chicken and pork, especially roasts.

Sweet fruitwoods—Apricot, plum, peach, nectarine: Great for fish and most white meats, including chicken, turkey, and pork.

259

10

WILD GAME

ALICE SPRINGS EMU STEAKS

Emu steaks, as well as other exotic meats (including alligator, caribou, frog, kangaroo, and rattlesnake), can be ordered on-line from Seattle's Finest Exotic Meats (at www.exoticmeats.com).

MARINADE

$\frac{1}{2}$ cup soy sauce

$\frac{1}{4}$ cup lime juice

2 tablespoons rice wine vinegar

$\frac{1}{4}$ cup orange juice

1 tablespoon brown sugar

1 tablespoon honey

1 teaspoon minced garlic

$\frac{1}{4}$ cup chopped scallions

$\frac{1}{2}$ teaspoon freshly ground ginger

1 teaspoon olive oil

Pinch of nutmeg

Sea salt to taste

Citrus pepper to taste

2 pounds emu steaks

2 to 3 tablespoons chilled butter

262

In a large bowl, whisk together all the marinade ingredients and pour into a Ziploc bag, add the emu steaks, and marinate them for 8 to 10 hours in the refrigerator.

Drain the meat, reserving the marinade, place the meat on a platter, cover with plastic wrap, and let it come to room temperature while you oil or spray the grill. Place an aluminum foil smoke packet on the coals (or medium gas flame) and when the wood chips begin to smoke, put the steaks on the grill.

In a medium saucepan over high heat, boil the remaining marinade for 10 minutes. Remove the pan from the heat and set it aside, keeping it warm over the lowest heat setting. Just before serving the emu, cut the butter into small chunks, add it to the sauce, and whisk into the mixture until smooth.

Grill the emu over medium coals or a gas fire (400° to 500°F) until medium rare, or 2 to 4 minutes per side.

Place the steaks on a heated platter, cover with foil, and let the meat rest for 2 to 3 minutes. Serve with the sauce on the side.

Serves 4

FRED'S APPLE/CHERRY-STUFFED PHEASANT

Fred and Dottie Anderson, Battle Creek, Michigan

Fred and Dottie gave me my first taste of pheasant one Thanksgiving, and we ate so much we literally had to lie down on the living room carpet for fear we'd explode if we so much as moved a finger. I have never forgotten the taste of those heavenly birds.

STUFFING

1 small tart apple

½ cup dried cherries

1 small onion, quartered

1 celery stalk, sliced

1 teaspoon dried rosemary

1 teaspoon poultry seasoning

½ teaspoon dried sage

1 tablespoon melted butter

2 tablespoons olive oil

One 4- to 5-pound pheasant, cleaned and
   checked for shot

Salt to taste

Pepper to taste

6 to 8 bacon slices (optional)

Core and chop the apple, place it in a small bowl, and set aside. Place the cherries in another small bowl and cover them with hot water. Soak for 20 minutes, then drain.

264

Mix the apples and cherries with the rest of the stuffing ingredients together in a medium bowl and set it aside.

Mix the melted butter and olive oil in a small bowl. Rub the bird down good with the butter-oil mixture, salt and pepper the bird inside and outside well, then stuff the cavity with the stuffing mixture.

Put the bird on an oiled grill rack in a shallow pan and add $\frac{1}{4}$ inch of water to keep the first juices from burning. Cook for 1 to $1\frac{1}{2}$ hours on medium-high heat (450° to 550°F), turning often. Check the pheasant after about 30 minutes and baste it again with the oil-butter mixture. Turn it over if the top starts to get too brown.

You can also cover it with bacon slices while it cooks. Remove when finished and discard the bacon.

Remove the pheasant from the grill, place it on a warm platter, cover it, and let it rest for 10 minutes before carving and serving.

Serves 2 to 4

BBQED VENISON LOIN CHOPS WITH APRICOT-MANGO CHUTNEY

BASTING SAUCE

3 teaspoons olive oil

2 garlic cloves, chopped

1 sprig rosemary

1 sprig thyme

2 teaspoons black peppercorns

Salt to taste

Pepper to taste

8 venison loin chops

Apricot-Mango Chutney (see recipe below)

266

In a small frying pan, place 1 teaspoon of the olive oil, then add the garlic and gently sauté over medium heat until the garlic browns, or 2 to 3 minutes. Add rosemary, thyme, and pepper and stir well.

Salt and pepper the venison loin chops. Brush the chops with the olive oil mixture. Place the chops on a grill heated to 400° to 500°F and grill for 4 to 5 minutes per side until the meat is cooked the way you like it, basting every time you turn the meat. Remove the chops from the grill, place on a heated platter, and let them rest for 2 minutes before serving.

Accompany the chops with warm apricot-mango chutney.

Serves 4

APRICOT-MANGO CHUTNEY

4 medium apricots, diced

3 medium mangoes, peeled and diced

8 ounces sugar

2 cups white wine vinegar

1 teaspoon cardamom

1 teaspoon powdered ginger

1 teaspoon salt

1 teaspoon white pepper

1 red bell pepper, finely diced

8 ounces golden raisins

$\frac{1}{2}$ cup finely diced red onion

$\frac{1}{4}$ cup minced shallots

Combine all of the ingredients in a large saucepan. Stir well and simmer, uncovered, for 45 minutes on low heat, or until the fruit is soft. Remove the chutney from the heat. Place in a small bowl and cool to room temperature. Pack the chutney in clean jars and refrigerate. Warm up in a small saucepan or microwave oven before serving with meat recipes. This chutney should last 3 to 4 days refrigerated.

267

Firin' up logs in hundred-foo

The cookin' Triola family, Houston.

Barbecuin' cowpokes take a break from the action in Houston.

...ncrete-block pits to cook whole sheep in Owensboro, Kentucky.

"I may forget my wife, I may forget my cigars, I may even forget where I am—but I always remembers the BBQ supply cupboard."
—A Columbus, Georgia, Pig Jig competitor

B&M'S NEW MEXICO
SMOKED WILD BOAR HAM

Bob and Marti Browne, Indianapolis, Indiana

"This recipe was inspired first by our love of wild game, and especially the discovery of the true pork flavor of wild boar. Friends tell us it is what pork used to taste like before it was sterilized, homogenized, and modernized. It was quite a revelation to our family, who loves it! Second was our passion for the vinegar-based barbecue sauces of the Carolinas. Finally, it was our passion for the flavors of northern New Mexico, the rich flavor of chilis used not for heat but for richness."

270

MARINADE

1 tablespoon olive oil

1 small white onion, finely chopped

3 garlic cloves, chopped

1 can chipotle peppers in adobo sauce, chopped

1 cup cider vinegar

1 cup dark molasses

12 ounces dark beer

2 tablespoons Pommery-style mustard

1 teaspoon dried Mexican oregano

$\frac{1}{2}$ teaspoon freshly ground black pepper

1 cup chopped cilantro

1 to 2 teaspoons mild chili powder

1 tablespoon ground cumin

1 teaspoon dried epazote (see Notes)

1 teaspoon dried sage

1 tablespoon onion powder

One 5- to 7-pound unsmoked bone-in boar
ham (see Notes)

SAUCE

2 cups ketchup (or tomato sauce)

1 roasted red bell pepper, skinned, seeded,
and pureed

1 cup tequila

Juice of 1 lime

Louisiana hot sauce

Salt to taste

OPTIONAL SPRAY

1 cup cider

$\frac{1}{4}$ cup balsamic vinegar

$\frac{1}{4}$ cup olive oil

Fresh cilantro for garnish

Heat the olive oil over low heat in a large sauté pan and then add the onion
and garlic and cook till the onions are translucent, 5 to 10 minutes. Add
the chipotle peppers in adobo sauce and cook for 2 minutes. Combine the
cooked mixture with all the other marinade ingredients (including
the cumin, epazote, sage, and onion powder) and simmer on low heat for 20
minutes, stirring occasionally. Remove the pan from the heat and let the
mixture cool. Place the ingredients in a blender or food processor and puree
until smooth.

Score the fat surface of the meat in two directions and puncture the meat all over with a serving fork. Place the meat in a large plastic bag or covered container and add the marinade; refrigerate it for 1 to 2 days, turning it several times per day.

Drain the meat and retain the marinade, pouring it into a large saucepan to boil for 10 minutes. Immediately turn the heat to low and add the ketchup or tomato sauce, red pepper puree, tequila, lime juice, hot sauce, and salt. Stir occasionally.

Simmer, covered, for 60 minutes over low heat, then simmer, uncovered, for 30 to 60 minutes until the sauce has reduced by one-third so it is a thick, syrupy liquid.

Prepare your smoker or barbecue grill with charcoal and soaked hardwood chunks (we prefer hickory and another wood such as maple, cherry, or apple) until a steady temperature of 200° to 250°F is reached. Place the ham on the smoker, or, if using a barbecue grill, on the cool side of the grill rack to cook over indirect heat.

Add a pan of water to the smoker to keep the meat moist. If your grill permits it, put the pan under the grill rack so it catches the drippings from the roast. The recirculating juices add to the flavor.

Smoke or grill the meat for approximately 10 to 12 hours (again using the smoker or indirect heating method), turning 3 to 4 times during the cooking cycle. If you wish, spray the cooking ham with a mixture of cider, balsamic vinegar, and olive oil each time before and after you turn the meat.

When finished, the meat should be nicely browned all over, and tender when pierced with a meat fork. Any juices should run clear.

Remove the meat from the grill, put it on a platter, and let it rest, covered in foil, for about 20 minutes, then slice it and serve on a large heated platter. Garnish with fresh cilantro. Drizzle the ham with sauce and serve the remaining sauce on the side.

Notes: Epazote is a strongly flavored herb that is commonly used in Mexican bean dishes, partly because it's supposed to reduce flatulence. Fresh epazote has dark green leaves with serrated edges.

The ham must be unsmoked. Shoulder or butt can be substituted, but wild boar has by far the best flavor range. If frozen, make sure the ham is thawed.

Serves 8 or more

GRILLED LOIN OF VENISON WITH WILD MUSHROOM RAGOUT

One 5- to 6-pound loin of venison

MARINADE

1 cup dry red wine

2 tablespoons olive oil

2 tablespoons soy sauce

1 teaspoon garlic powder

1 teaspoon liquid smoke

Juice of 1 lemon

$\frac{1}{2}$ teaspoon black pepper

6 slices apple-smoked bacon, thick cut

BASTING SAUCE

1 cup red wine

$\frac{1}{2}$ cup olive oil

1 tablespoon cider vinegar

Mushroom Ragout (see page 274)

1 small bunch rosemary for garnish

1 small bunch marjoram for garnish

Remove the white, shiny muscle sheath from the outside of the loin, and cut a $\frac{3}{4}$-inch-deep slit down the full length of the meat. Mix the marinade in a large plastic bag, add the loin, and store it overnight in the refrigerator.

Prepare a barbecue for indirect heat with a water pan (see page 6) at medium-high heat (450° to 550°F). Make long slits across the loin and stuff the bacon strips in the slits. Cook the meat approximately 15 to 20 minutes per pound to desired doneness (like prime rib, the rarer the better). Mix the basting sauce in a medium bowl and baste the loin every 10 to 15 minutes during cooking.

When the meat is done, remove it from the grill, let it rest covered for 10 minutes, then serve it on a bed of mushroom ragout. Garnish with fresh sprigs of rosemary and marjoram.

Serves 4 to 6

MUSHROOM RAGOUT

274

3 pounds fresh wild mushrooms
　　(shiitake, chanterelle, oyster, morel,
　　and straw varieties)
1 medium onion, chopped
1 stick butter
2 tablespoons olive oil
$\frac{3}{4}$ cup red wine
Juice of $\frac{1}{2}$ lemon
Pinch of marjoram

While the meat is cooking, sauté the ragout ingredients in a large cast-iron skillet, over medium-high heat, stirring constantly, until most of the liquid is gone, or 10 to 15 minutes.

Serve alongside venison or other game or fowl.

MAPLE PECAN-STUFFED RABBIT, EH?

Bruce Jacobson, Swine Fellows Barbecue Team, Brantford, Ontario, Canada

In 1999, the Swine Fellows won First Place in the Cooking from the Home Land Contest at the Jack Daniel's World Invitational Barbecue Competition, in Lynchburg, Tennessee, using this smoked rabbit recipe. They won the competition in 2000, 2001, and 2002 with different recipes.

1 cup pure maple syrup

1 cup finely chopped pecans

1 tablespoon prepared mustard

1 teaspoon ground allspice

Pinch of salt and pepper

3 pounds rabbit, deboned

5 strips bacon

1 apple, peeled and sliced

Start the charcoal in the smoker or barbecue and bring the temperature to 200° to 225°F.

Mix evenly the maple syrup, pecans, mustard, allspice, salt, and pepper in a glass bowl, and cover the bowl. Let the mixture stand for 48 hours at room temperature. Drain in a colander and reserve the liquid in a small bowl for basting. Save the pecan mixture for the stuffing.

Place the larger shoulder cuts of the rabbit together, then lay the rest of the deboned meat on top in a rectangle. Spread the pecan stuffing on top of the meat, then roll the meat around it and wrap the bacon strips around the rabbit. Use wooden skewers to hold it all together.

275

Lunchtime at Jack's Bar-B-Q, Nashville, Tennessee.

Using the indirect cooking method, place the rabbit on the rack away from the heat. Baste with some of the reserved maple syrup liquid. Place the apple slices on the rack beside the rabbit. Using 1 cup water-soaked wood chips, start smoking or grill-smoking the rabbit, adding 1 cup wood chips every half hour for the first 3 hours. Continue basting the rabbit every half hour.

Cook the rabbit until the internal temperature is 165°F, or 4 to 6 hours depending on the smoker or barbecue.

When the rabbit is done, remove it from the barbecue and wrap it in aluminum foil. Allow it to sit for 20 minutes before slicing. Carefully remove the wooden skewers and discard. Slice the rabbit about 1 inch thick and stack offset on a platter, placing apple slices between the meat slices. Baste the rabbit and apples one more time with the maple syrup baste for presentation.

Serves 4

OL' BILL'S TERIYAKI ELK STEAKS

Bill Kelly, Woodland, Washington

This simple recipe may be expanded with veggies and mushrooms and brushed with marinade to make great shish kebabs, or you can cook just the meat as premain-course finger food. It works well with all sorts of dark-meat game, including duck and goose. We've even had success with wild turkey (the feathered kind, as well as the bottled variety!). If you're using turkey or chicken, just marinate it for 20 to 30 minutes before grilling.

1 pound elk or deer venison (round steak
   or shoulder cuts)

1 cup brown sugar
1 cup your favorite commercial teriyaki marinade
1 teaspoon garlic salt or minced garlic to taste
One 4-foot-long willow switch (see Note)

277

Cut the meat into 1-inch cubes. In a large bowl, dissolve the brown sugar in the marinade, and mix in the garlic. Add the meat and marinate, covered, for 2 to 3 hours. Place it on skewers and set the skewers on a hot barbecue grill (500° to 600°F) for about 2 minutes per side—don't overcook it.

Note: Stay close to your grill with a willow switch while cooking. Guests tend to sneak samples off the skewers. Use the switch sparingly, but with authority.

Serves 4 to 8

TERIYAKI BUFFALO RIB EYES

Bozeman Trail Wagon Train

Cooked by the wagon train cook over a hardwood fire as we made camp under the stars in the Sawtooth Mountains. Serve buffalo rib-eye steaks with barbecued beans, barbecued corn on the cob, and Indian fry bread.

278

2 tablespoons soy sauce

1 garlic clove, minced or pressed

2 tablespoons brown sugar

1 teaspoon ground ginger

2 tablespoons lemon juice

3 tablespoons olive oil

1 tablespoon minced onion

$\frac{1}{4}$ teaspoon black pepper

1 tablespoon McCormick Montreal steak seasoning

4 buffalo rib-eye steaks, 12 ounces each

Combine the soy sauce, garlic, brown sugar, ginger, lemon juice, olive oil, onion, pepper, and steak seasoning. Pour it over the steak, in a wide, flat Pyrex dish. Cover with plastic wrap and refrigerate for 6 hours or (much, much better) till the next day.

Lift the steaks from the marinade and drain briefly. Save the marinade and boil it for 10 minutes in a small saucepan, over high heat. Place the rib eyes on a barbecue and grill them for 6 to 8 minutes over a medium-hot fire (450° to 550°F) for medium rare, turning once and basting with the boiled reserved marinade.

Serves 4 *big* eaters, or 8 small ones

QUE'N AT THE RITZ

How to Know If You're in a Good or Bad BBQ Joint

THE ENTRANCE

Scene A: The front door is unpainted, broken, hanging on one hinge, and has Band-Aids covering rips in the screen. There are three bullet holes through the doorjamb. Or maybe it doesn't even have a door. "Welcum to Bubba's," says a hand-painted sign.

Scene B: The front door is carved from rare woods, has a polished brass handle, and has a uniformed doorman standing by it to open it for you. "Bienvenue à Chez Barbeque Magnifique."

THE STAFF

Scene A: You're greeted by a 5-foot-2-inch-tall man who's as wide as he is tall, wearing the remaining frayed wisps of a stained tank top, a three-year-old torn paper frycook's hat, and rubber thongs. Hard to understand what he's saying because he is chomping on a 2-inch-long remnant of a bad cigar.

Scene B: The doorman introduces you to the maître d', Pierre, who's dressed up like Fred Astaire, including the top hat, cane, and spats, and who asks if you have reservations, disdainfully dissecting your net worth in one glance. You should have worn the Guccis, or at least the DKNY. When his monocled eye finds your name, he claps daintily and sashays around the desk. "We have a special table set aside tonight, monsieur, in the Renaissance Room."

THE TABLE

Scene A: You're seated at a Formica-topped table, which had to have been stolen off the *Sanford & Son* set, one metal leg broken but held up by an upended tomato juice can, cobwebs dangling from the underside, a sticky substance on one corner gathering a marching band of ants, and another corner chewed away, with obvious teeth marks. As you sit down, you slip on a puddle of either blood or BBQ sauce (you hope it's the latter). Two dead flowers, and some sort of green thing droops out of a cracked beer bottle. None of the chairs could have cost more than $1.99 and none match. Not just at your table, but in the entire room.

Charlie Vergos, one of the world's greatest
BBQ pioneers, at his restaurant in Memphis;
the legendary back alley BBQ haven, Rendezvous.

Lunchtime crowds jam the Goode Company Restaurant in Houston.

Back of the house: as funky as it gets, at Arthur Bryant's in Kansas City.

Scene B: You're guided down a carpeted foyer into a dining room that looks like Liberace decorated it, and are seated at a table covered with white linen, Baccarat crystal, and a bouquet of perfect salmon pink and ivory roses. The chandelier could have been used in the palace of Versailles, the sterling silver probably came from Buckingham Palace, and the chairs are better than you have in your living room. In fact, they're probably better than those at Buckingham Palace, too. You drop a pen and can't find it in the two-inch-thick antique Persian pile.

THE ATMOSPHERE

Scene A: After noting the quaint ambience of neon beer signs, 1950s tool shop calendars adorned with partially clothed "models," multicolored strands of ceiling-mounted flypaper (many of which are moving due to the heavy population of flies entrapped thereon), and a rotating floor-mounted fan that alternatively emits a loud hum or a sound not unlike metal pieces being shoved through a meat grinder. The busboy tosses you a flyswatter, "just in case."

Scene B: The five-piece orchestral group begins a selection of Strauss waltzes as you are being seated. The collection of classical and contemporary paintings, on loan from the Metropolitan Museum of Art, and which has been featured in *Gourmet* magazine, is perfectly set off by the French lace curtains and Viennese velvet draperies. Your waiter, actually you discover it's your waiter's "first assistant," glides by and welcomes you as he hands your lady a perfect red rose, whispering, "Bon appetit."

THE MENU

Scene A: As you search vainly for a menu, finally asking the now-belching busboy for help, you discover "there ain't one, Bub," as he delicately points with a hangnailed middle finger (the rest on that hand are missing) toward a chalkboard of "Daily Specialz." You think you'll have the "brisket" of beef, ribs, fries, white bread, and sauce. After all, that's all there is.

Scene B: A white gloved hand appears from nowhere and hands you a leather and velvet menu folder, engraved with the name of the restaurant in 24-karat gold leaf. Inside, a parchment manuscript adorned with perfect calligraphy announces the soup, salads, entrées, vegetables, starches, and desserts. But only your menu has prices, the menu given to the ladies has small violets where the prices should be. It takes you 20 minutes to read the 164 items, and you haven't even looked at the "Surprise du Chef" page inserted in the middle.

THE MEAL

Scene A: The food arrives at last, plunked on a piece of butcher paper. A massive pile of pork ribs and a Volkswagen-sized hunk of black-as-a-meteor beef sit steaming under the waving flypaper strands. The chef, excuse me, pitman, grabs a handful of French fries directly out of a basket still dripping with hot lard, takes half a loaf of bread from the Wonder wrapper, and throws in a half handful of pickle slices. When you ask about an accompanying sauce, he mumbles, "What ya kiddin? It's on da table already!" You quickly retrieve the sauce from the garbage can, where you had heaved it, thinking it was a leftover, unfinished bottle of very cheap beer.

Scene B: After deciding on the Barbeque Kobe Beef (flown in that day from Nagasaki, Japan), the Smoked Pork riblets from New Zealand, the Patates Frites du Belgique, and the Moët & Chandon barbecue sauce (vintage 1954), you watch as the food is delivered on Louis XIV sterling silver platters by a platoon of waitpersons. In perfect unison the plates are placed in front of each diner, and the warming lids lifted with the precision of a symphony orchestra. One tuxedoed lass runs up with a golden plate adorned with imported French cornichons and slips it on the table.

THE BIG (OR NOT-SO-BIG) EVENT

Scene A: There is no conversation at the table now. Guttural grunts, moans, sighs, lip smacks, and the sound of ripping flesh obliterates even the Grandpa Jones, Roy Acuff, and Tex Ritter records playing on the jukebox. Flying fingers grab ribs, hunks of brisket, slopping brick red sauce on white bread and using the sopping mass to fashion gooey sandwiches of beef. Rib bones fly like drumsticks at a Buddy Rich drum concert. Gurgles of beer, slurps of sauce, appropriate and inappropriate body-cavity sounds bounce off the linoleum as the four crazed barbecue fanatics go at it full boar. Finally, as the food vanishes into sauce-stained mouths, an eerie quiet ensues. Now only faint sighs and the sound of wet naps being released from foil packages mar the otherwise quiet room. The paltry bill was paid with pocket change. The fan has finally died, Tex Ritter has faded into the night, and peace has settled at Bubba's.

Scene B: After finding a rib bearing a piteous 1/4-inch of fibrous meat under a 2-inch-thick layer of tepid, tasteless sauce, and after what seemed an hour masticating an immolated chunk of beef (or was it snow tire), which was painfully swallowed in an esophagus-stretching gulp; and after the limpid fried potatoes swimming in precious oils and vintage Belgian mayonnaise were sadly pushed aside, the feast began, and an entire plate of pickles (excuse me, cornichons) were frantically gobbled up as the only really edible food items on the table. Oh yes, the water was okay too, except for the damnable lemon-in-netting floating between the Greenland Glacier ice cubes. Groans, growls, and gnashing of teeth followed as the itemized bill, the computation of which certainly would tax a mainframe computer, and which totaled slightly less than the latest contract for a fully loaded Boeing 777, was delivered by yet another gloved hand holding yet another gilded platter. As the orchestra packed up to go, the chandelier dimmed, the rose petals fluttered to the floor, and our still-ravenous dinner party voted unanimously to adjourn to another local eatery: A new Que joint down the street . . . Bubba's!

The moral of these stories: Fancy names, white linen, and astronomical prices do not good BBQ guarantee. Rather savor and relish the wise expenditure of money, passion, and time on the quality of the Que itself. Leave the tables to Formica, the floors to Linoleum, and the dinnerware to Chinette. The BBQ belongs to Bubba!

283

11 DESSERTS

"HEDDO" BAKED APPLES

Grandma Welch, Hartford, Connecticut

Grandma Welch was a mere wisp of a woman who delighted all with her smile, her endless cheer, her boundless love for everyone and everything, and her love of good food (as long as she didn't have to cook it).

$\frac{1}{4}$ cup currants

4 large Golden Delicious apples,
$\frac{1}{2}$ pound each

$\frac{1}{4}$ cup maple syrup
(the real stuff, please!)

$\frac{1}{4}$ cup golden raisins

$\frac{1}{4}$ cup brown sugar, packed

$\frac{1}{2}$ cup crushed graham crackers

$\frac{1}{2}$ teaspoon curry powder

Dash of cinnamon

4 large pats of butter

Prepare the barbecue for indirect heat (see page 6) at 400° to 500°F.

Place the currants in a small bowl and cover with hot water. Soak for 20 minutes.

Wash and core the apples, leave at least a $\frac{1}{2}$-inch core hole. Mix the maple syrup, raisins, brown sugar, currants, graham crackers, curry powder, and cinnamon well in a medium bowl, and stuff tightly into the apple cores with a small spoon.

Place a water pan on the cool side of the grill (see page 6). Place each apple on a square of aluminum foil and top it with a butter pat. Seal the foil and place the apples on the grill on the side above the water pan. Bake them on the grill for 1 to $1\frac{1}{4}$ hours, or until tender.

Remove from the heat, unwrap the apples, and serve immediately.

Serves 4

ARNOLD'S SOUSED PEACHES

6 peaches, firm but ripe

$\frac{3}{4}$ cup Grand Marnier

1 teaspoon vanilla extract

2 tablespoons dark brown sugar

TOPPING

$1\frac{1}{4}$ cups mascarpone cheese

6 shortbread cookies, crushed

$\frac{1}{2}$ cup Grand Marnier

12 shortbread cookies

Halve the peaches and discard the pits. Do not peel the peaches. Mix the Grand Marnier, vanilla, and the brown sugar together in a shallow, wide bowl and place the peaches in it flesh side down. Cover with plastic wrap, and allow them to soak for 3 to 4 hours.

Prepare a grill for indirect heat (see page 6) at 300° to 350°F. Place the peaches on the oiled grill away from the heat. Cook them flesh side down, for 6 to 8 minutes, or until grill marks appear, then turn them over and cook for 5 to 8 minutes more until the second side has grill marks and the peaches are soft.

About 5 minutes before the peaches are done, mix together the mascarpone and the cookies in a medium bowl, cover and refrigerate until ready to use. This is best done no earlier than 5 minutes before serving, otherwise the biscuits will be very soggy.

When the peaches are done remove them from the grill with a large slotted spoon or spatula. Place 2 halves on each plate; place a spoonful of the mascarpone into each hollow, and pour a bit of Grand Marnier over the dessert.

Place 2 shortbread cookies on each plate alongside the peaches and serve.

Serves 6

287

BBQ 'MERICUN APPLE PIE

Jerry Soucy is the founder of the Pig and Pepper Barbecue Harvest, a KCBS-sanctioned event held each October to determine the Massachusetts State Barbecue Champion. Founded in 1991, Pig and Pepper is the first, largest, and longest-running KCBS-sanctioned barbecue cookoff in New England, and has raised over $250,000 for charity. Jerry lives near Boston with his wife, two teenage children, and a battered old kettle grill named "Sputnik." When the pie is ready to serve (still warm), enhance the presentation with a garnish of bright autumn leaves or fresh berries. Serve with ice cream, or traditional extra-sharp Cheddar cheese the way New Englanders like it.

290

Your favorite piecrust recipe, or
1 package of a frozen,
ready-to-use pie crust
3 pounds apples (Macouns,
Empires, or Granny Smiths),
peeled and sliced
Sugar to taste
Cinnamon to taste
2 tablespoons lemon juice (optional)
2 tablespoons unsalted butter
Light cream for brushing the crust

Build a fire for indirect cooking (see page 6) or if using gas, only turn on the burners on one side of the grill, to reach a temperature of 350° to

400°F. Place the water pan on the opposite side of the grill. Cover the cooker to control the fire, watching to be sure that it does not become too hot (use the oven thermometer or place your hand carefully over the grill and count, to make sure the temperature does not go above 400°F (see page 11 for checking the heat this way).

Prepare your pie dough in advance, wrapping the ball of dough tightly in plastic wrap or wax paper and keeping it refrigerated until you are ready to roll it out.

Peel and slice your apples into a large bowl, and toss with sugar and cinnamon until the pieces are well coated. You can also use a squirt of fresh lemon to keep the apples from turning brown or if you find the whole mix is too sweet.

On a piece of aluminum foil that has been lightly dusted with flour, roll out the pie dough into a single large circle—larger than you normally would if you were going to put this crust in a pie plate.

Mound the seasoned apples in the center of the crust, then fold the edges of the crust toward the middle of the mound. You will end up with an open inner circle of exposed apples, and the whole thing will look sort of like a tart but with more top crust. Dot the open area with small pieces of the butter, and brush the top crust with the light cream. Finish by sprinkling some additional sugar over the pie.

Slide the pie onto the grill, keeping the foil in place for ease of handling. Cover the cooker.

Add lit charcoal as required to maintain the cooker temperature at 350° to 400°F for 35 to 40 minutes, or until the top crust has browned and the filling is bubbly. We used a flashlight to monitor the progress through the vent holes, to avoid raising the cover and losing the heat.

When the pie is done, transfer it onto a cutting board or other surface, sliding it off the foil to cool. While you may be tempted to just dig right in, the filling of a pie right out of the cooker may be dangerously hot. A brief cooling period also helps the juices to settle and the filling to firm up, resulting in neater cuts and a better presentation. Wait at least 15 minutes to let the pie cool and firm up. Serve warm.

Serves 4 to 8

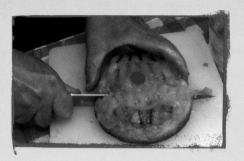

FIJIAN BARBECUED PINEAPPLE

½ cup orange honey

½ cup butter

½ cup dark brown sugar

2 tablespoons water

½ cup dark rum

294

1 pineapple, cored and cut into
   8 vertical wedges

1 pint coconut ice cream

Combine the honey, butter, brown sugar, water, and rum in a medium saucepan. Bring to a boil, over high heat, stirring constantly. Reduce the heat to low and simmer until the sauce begins to thicken, about 10 minutes. Remove the sauce from the heat and allow it to cool.

Preheat the grill to a medium-hot fire (450° to 550°F) and oil the grill. Using a long-handled pastry brush, coat the pineapple pieces with the sauce and place them on the grill. Cook them for about 5 minutes, turning occasionally, until the edges of the pineapple brown. The surface of the pineapple should brown as well.

Remove the pineapple from the grill, serve immediately with ice cream and the remaining sauce.

Serves 8

FLAMIN' GOL-DURN BANANAS

6 tablespoons butter

¾ cup dark brown sugar

6 bananas, very new and hard, peeled,
    sliced in half lengthwise

1 tablespoon ground cinnamon

1 teaspoon ground nutmeg

¾ cup dark rum

¼ cup banana liqueur

Vanilla ice cream

295

Preheat the grill to a medium-hot fire (400° to 500°F) using the indirect method (see page 6). Melt the butter in a cast-iron skillet on the hot side of the grill, then add the brown sugar, stirring well to dissolve it. Add the bananas, sprinkle with the cinnamon and nutmeg, and sauté gently over the cooler side of the grill until golden brown on both sides, 10 minutes.

Take the pan off the grill and place it on a heat pad on the table or countertop. Slowly pour the rum and liqueur over the bananas. Carefully ignite the liqueur with a long match or BBQ charcoal lighter, using a large spoon to baste the bananas with the flaming liquor (see Note).

Serve over ice cream when the flame dies out, which should take only a few seconds.

Note: Caution is the rule whenever liquor is to be flamed—you must *always* remove the pan from the heat source when adding liquor.

Serves 6

FRAU BLAU'S CHOCOLATE CAKE WITH SMOKY CHOCOLATE FROSTING

CAKE

6 ounces all-purpose flour

1 ounce cocoa

1 level teaspoon baking powder

5 ounces light brown sugar, soft

2 eggs, separated

6 tablespoons salad oil

4 tablespoons cream

1 teaspoons vanilla extract

6 tablespoons dark rum

Smoky Chocolate Frosting (see recipe below)

296

Preheat the smoker or BBQ kettle to 350°F for indirect cooking (see page 6). Thoroughly grease with Crisco or butter an 8-inch round cake tin. Sift the flour, cocoa, and baking powder into a medium bowl. Stir in the brown sugar. Add the egg yolks, oil, cream, vanilla, and rum, and beat to a smooth batter using a hand or electric mixer.

In a separate bowl, whip the egg whites to soft peaks and fold into the batter with a large metal spoon. Transfer the mixture to a prepared round cake tin and bake it in a hot barbecue grill or smoker (on indirect heat) for $1\frac{1}{4}$ hours until the cake has fully risen, is golden, and a skewer or toothpick inserted into the middle comes out clean.

Remove the cake from the barbecue. Leave it for 10 minutes, then turn it out onto a wire cake rack. Let the cake cool completely. Meanwhile, prepare the frosting.

Serves 8

SMOKY CHOCOLATE FROSTING

2 pounds semisweet chocolate

1 pint fresh whipping cream

6 ounces light rum

Grate the chocolate into a medium stainless-steel mixing bowl. Add the cream and stir.

Place the bowl in a smoker and smoke at 220°F for 30 minutes. Stir the mixture every 15 minutes. For a heavier smoke flavor increase the smoking time by 15 minutes. If the chocolate mixture is not completely melted after 30 minutes, place it over a pot of boiling water and bring up to 160°F; whisk until smooth and add the light rum, then whisk until smooth again.

When the frosting is smooth, remove the bowl from the heat with oven mitts. Let the frosting cool thoroughly. When you are ready to frost the cake, beat the frosting until fluffy with a hand mixer and then smooth it over the cake.

297

GRILLED PEARS AND APPLES WITH MANGO RELISH

2 large pears, ripe but firm, cut
   into 1-inch chunks

2 apples, cut into eighths

8 tablespoons preserved ginger syrup

4 tablespoons rice wine vinegar

4 tablespoons olive oil

MANGO RELISH

2 mangoes, diced

2 tablespoons chopped shallots

$\frac{1}{4}$ teaspoon ground ginger

2 tablespoons chopped fresh mint leaves

2 teaspoons olive oil

Preheat the grill to 350° to 400°F. Place bamboo skewers in a flat glass pan and cover with hot water. Weight them down with a full water glass or bottle and allow them to soak for 20 minutes.

Thread the pears and apples onto the soaked wooden skewers. In a small bowl, combine the ginger syrup, vinegar, and olive oil, and stir until well blended. Grill the skewers, brushing them frequently with the ginger syrup mixture until lightly browned and crisp, about 10 minutes.

While the pears and apples are cooking, in a small bowl, combine the relish ingredients, stir well to mix thoroughly, and place in a small bowl. Serve at room temperature alongside the pear-apple skewers.

298

Serves 4

KATIE'S 180 CHEESECAKE

Katie Lane, Austin, Texas

This recipe took first place in desserts at the Jack Daniel's Cookoff a few years ago. The cheesecake recipe is called "Katie's 180" for the perfect scores it garnered: 10s in each of the appearance, taste, and texture categories—from all six judges! Wow!

$1\frac{1}{2}$ cups vanilla wafer crumbs

6 tablespoons melted butter

1 tablespoon Gentleman Jack whiskey

One 14-ounce package caramels

One 5-ounce can evaporated milk

1 generous cup coarsely chopped
   nuts (I use pecans)

Three 8-ounce packages softened
   cream cheese

3 eggs at room temperature

1 teaspoon vanilla extract

$\frac{1}{2}$ cup sugar

1 can Eagle Brand sweetened
   condensed milk

$\frac{1}{2}$ cup melted chocolate chips

Spray the sides of a 9-inch springform pan with nonstick spray and dust with half of the vanilla wafer crumbs. Mix the excess crumbs with the melted butter and the Gentleman Jack whiskey. Stir together and press into the bottom and $\frac{1}{2}$ inch up the sides of the pan. Set the pan aside.

Slowly, and over low heat, melt the caramels and evaporated milk together in a medium saucepan, stirring occasionally, about 5 minutes. When the mixture is completely melted, pour it over the crust. Sprinkle the chopped nuts over the caramel mixture.

Using an electric mixer, mix the cream cheese, eggs, vanilla, and sugar together until smooth. Add the condensed milk and mix well. Add the melted chocolate and blend completely with the mixer. Carefully pour this mixture over the top of the nuts and, using a toothpick or a sharp knife, try to get out all the air bubbles.

Bake the cheesecake for 45 minutes in a 350°F smoker or barbecue grill over indirect heat with a water pan under the cheesecake (see page 9). The cheesecake should appear golden brown on top and be firm to the touch. Remove it from the heat and cool completely.

Serves 12 to 14

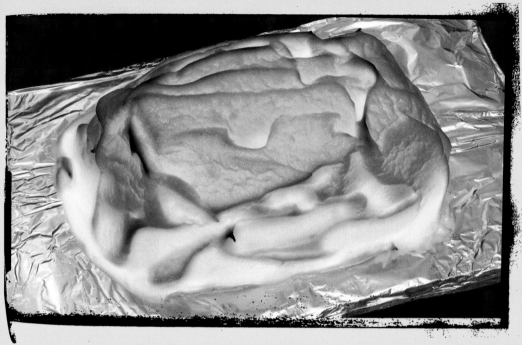

300

RB'S BARBECUED ICE CREAM (A.K.A. GRILLED ALASKA)

12 to 16 egg whites

1 teaspoon cream of tartar

1 cup granulated sugar

Chocolate sprinkles

1 standard-size pound cake, frozen

1 gallon high-quality ice cream,
   frozen hard

One 8-ounce jar chocolate
   fudge sauce

1 small bunch fresh mint leaves
   for garnish

Take one wooden plank, 12 × 12 × 1-inch thick, and wrap it in two to three layers of heavy-duty aluminum foil.

Get a good hot fire (600° to 700°F plus) going in a grill or smoker. If you use charcoal or briquettes in a grill, cover the bottom of the grill pan with the charcoal. If using a gas grill, turn on all the burners to high.

Using an electric mixer or hand beater, whip the egg whites, cream of tartar, and sugar into a very stiff meringue, so that when you pull the beaters away, sharp points stand up in the meringue. At the last minute, add a generous amount of chocolate sprinkles and quickly fold them into the egg whites. Put the meringue mixture in the refrigerator until ready to use.

Set the foil-wrapped board on the counter. Working quickly, use a sharp serrated knife to cut the frozen pound cake in half horizontally, and lay one half on the foil.

Open the carton of ice cream and cut a $\frac{1}{2}$-inch to 3-inch slice lengthwise off the brick of ice cream. Place the slice of ice cream on the cake. If the ice cream is not completely covering the bottom slice of the cake, cut another $\frac{1}{2}$-inch to 3-inch slice and fit it alongside so you have an even layer over the cake. Sprinkle more chocolate sprinkles on the ice cream and cover it with the top half of the cake.

Using a flexible spatula, completely cover the cake on all sides with the meringue, being sure to bring the meringue all the way down to *touch the foil* all around the cake. If you leave any gaps, the ice cream may melt and spoil the dessert.

Place the plank in the center of the grill or smoker and immediately close the cover. Check it after 2 minutes and as soon as you see the peaks of meringue turning brown, remove the dessert from the cooker. This will only take 4 to 5 minutes with a very hot fire.

Slide the cake off the plank and onto a chilled serving platter. With a heated, serrated knife, cut vertical slices through the meringue, cake, and ice cream, and put the slices on plates onto which you have spooned a generous pool of chocolate sauce.

Garnish the sauce with fresh mint leaves, shake more sprinkles over the meringue, and serve immediately.

Serves 4 to 6

302

SOMEBUNNY'S CHOCOLATE BANANA BOATS

4 to 6 green bananas (underripe
    bananas are best)
1 to 2 large milk chocolate bars,
    broken into $\frac{1}{4}$- to $\frac{1}{2}$-inch pieces,
    or 1 small 11-ounce bag
    milk chocolate morsels
1 tablespoon dark rum (optional)

Lay the bananas on their side and with a sharp knife slit them from end to end, deep into the banana, but not cutting through the bottom peel.

Spread the slits wide and stuff with the pieces of chocolate. The amount you put into each banana is usually determined by the amount of chocolate or the number of people eating the treats.

Wrap the bananas in aluminum foil. Place them on the grill over medium heat (350° to 400°F) for about 10 minutes, or until the chocolate is melted and the bananas are partially cooked. Remove the foil from the bananas, then carefully cut away the top section of the peel, and scoop out the chocolate and fruit from the resulting banana "boat" with a spoon.

For true decadence, place a large scoop of vanilla ice cream beside the banana boat and dig in. If you wish to sin even more, pour 1 tablespoon dark rum over the bananas.

Serves 4 to 6

MISS ABIGAIL'S GRILLED NECTARINES

4 large nectarines (or peaches), cut in half

$1\frac{1}{2}$ ounces butter, melted

3 tablespoons brown sugar

Two 8-ounce containers lemon yogurt

Dash of cinnamon

Dash of nutmeg

303

Place the nectarines in a medium cast-iron dish, cut side up, and brush them with the butter. Scatter half the brown sugar over the fruit and grill over high heat (450° to 550°F) for 8 to 10 minutes until the sugar caramelizes.

Leaving the dish on the grill, place a large spoonful of lemon yogurt on top of each nectarine, sprinkle with the remaining brown sugar, cinnamon, and nutmeg, and grill for another 3 minutes.

Remove the nectarines from the heat and let them stand for 3 minutes before serving.

Can be served with fresh vanilla ice cream or fruit sorbet.

Serves 4

TO DI FOR BERRY-CHERRY NUT COBBLER

Diana Dillard, Lakeshore, Washington

Diana is a graduate of the Culinary Institute of America, former owner/executive chef at Rain City Grill in Seattle (which was voted one of the top five restaurants in the city), a freelance culinary consultant, and currently teaches professional culinary arts courses at Seattle Culinary Academy at Seattle Central Community College.

304

FRUIT FILLING

$1\frac{1}{2}$ cups raspberries, fresh or
   frozen and thawed
1 cup blueberries, fresh or
   frozen and thawed
1 cup sweet cherries, pitted, fresh
   or frozen and thawed
$\frac{1}{4}$ cup granulated sugar
1 tablespoon cornstarch
2 teaspoons fresh lemon juice

TOPPING

$\frac{3}{4}$ cup all-purpose flour
$\frac{1}{4}$ cup brown sugar
2 tablespoons confectioners' sugar
$\frac{1}{4}$ teaspoon salt
$\frac{1}{4}$ teaspoon baking powder
$\frac{1}{4}$ teaspoon ground cinnamon
$\frac{1}{4}$ teaspoon ground nutmeg
$\frac{1}{2}$ cup coarsely chopped walnuts
$\frac{1}{3}$ cup butter, melted

Preheat the smoker or barbecue to 350° to 400°F for indirect heating (see page 6).

Lightly butter an 8-inch cake pan. Gently rinse the berries and cherries. Drain on a paper towel–lined cookie sheet to absorb the moisture.

Place the berries and cherries in a medium mixing bowl. In a separate small bowl, combine the sugar and cornstarch and sprinkle over the berry mixture. Add the lemon juice and toss gently. Transfer to the prepared cake pan.

Sift together the flour, sugars, salt, baking powder, cinnamon, and nutmeg. Add the walnuts. Pour in the butter and toss the ingredients with a fork to form large crumbs. Sprinkle the topping over the berry and cherry fruit filling with a large spoon.

Bake the cobbler for approximately 30 minutes, or until the crumbs begin to brown and the filling juices are bubbling. Serve slightly warm or at room temperature topped with whipped cream or ice cream.

Serves 4 to 6

TRICIA'S PINEAPPLE, RAISIN, AND PLUM UPSIDE-DOWN THING

$\frac{1}{4}$ cup butter

$\frac{3}{4}$ cup dark brown sugar

1 can pineapple chunks, drained

$\frac{1}{2}$ cup golden raisins

12 dried plums, pits removed

1 box lemon (or orange) cake mix,
   (e.g. Betty Crocker SuperMoist Lemon
   cake mix, which additionally requires
   $1\frac{1}{4}$ cups water, $\frac{1}{3}$ cup vegetable oil,
   and 3 large eggs)

1 pint whipping cream for garnish

1 to 2 tablespoons confectioners' sugar

1 teaspoon vanilla extract

306

Mix the butter and brown sugar together in a bowl with a fork until they form flakelike pieces. Spread this mixture evenly across the bottom of a aluminum foil pan.

Place the fruit on top of the butter-sugar mixture, alternating layers: pineapple, then raisins, then plums.

Follow the instructions on the box for mixing the lemon (or orange) cake and, after mixing, pour it over the pan of fruit.

Mounding the coals on one side of the barbecue, place a water pan on the other side, replace the grill rack, and put the cake on the side away from the coals (indirect heat).

The temperature should be around 300° to 350°F. Keep the barbecue lid closed as much as possible. The cake is ready when a toothpick inserted into the middle comes out clean, usually 30 to 35 minutes.

Remove the cake from the heat and cool for 15 minutes. While the cake is cooling use an electric mixer to whip the cream, adding the confectioners' sugar and vanilla while whipping. Then turn the cake over on a platter and serve each piece with a large dollop of fresh whipped cream on the side.

Serves 8

THE OFFICIAL BARBECUE JUDGES' OATH OF OFFICE

I do solemnly swear to objectively and subjectively evaluate each barbecue meat that is presented to my eyes—to my nose—to my hands—and to my palate.

I accept my duty as a barbecue judge, so that
Truth,
Justice,
Excellence in barbecue,
and the American way of life,
is strengthened and preserved forever!
You're on your oath!

—Remus Powers, Ph.B. (a.k.a. Ardie Davis)

ThanQUEs

OUR SPECIAL THANKS TO THE FOLLOWING CORPORATIONS, FOR THEIR ASSISTANCE, ENTHUSIASTIC SUPPORT, AND HELP IN MAKING THIS BOOK HAPPEN:

Char-Broil
McCormick Spices
BIC Corporation
Georgie Boy Manufacturing

AND TO THE FOLKS AT:

Blue Mountain Design Works
Bruce Foods Corporation
Canadian Bison Association
Cash & Carry
Chefwear
Estes Clothiers

KitchenAid
Louisiana Hot Sauce
The National Park Board
Oregon Cedar Grill
Oregon Spice Company
OXO International

Smart & Final Stores Corporation
Sur la Table, Portland, Oregon
The Real Canadian Bacon Company
Wells Lamont

A HEARTY AND HEARTFELT THANQUE TO THE PEOPLE WHO HELPED ME IN MY PASSION TO SEARCH OUT AND SHARE THE BEST BARBECUE I COULD FIND.

Alison Bitner, Sur la Table
Aliza Fogelson, ReganBooks
All-American Smokers, Leesburg, Georgia
Allen Erkhart & the Grill Masters Team, Americus, Georgia
Anne and Terry Callon
Ardie Davis, a.k.a. Remus Powers
Arthur Peterson, Char-Broil
Barbara Johnson
Barry Pelts, Jan Klein, Corky's Ribs & BBQ, Memphis, Tennessee
BBQfan1
BBQ'N Fools
Betsy Sunden, Bayer Corporation
Bill and Pam Medlock, Cow-a-Bunga
BJ Hockman, Oregon Spice Company
Bob Hastings, Rockland Area C of C
Bob and Debbie Morris
Bob, Marti, Rick, and Anne Browne

Bray Vincent, Goode Company
Brea Lang
Brette & Lindy Harte
Brian Campbell
Brian Murphy
Bruce Jacobson, Canadian Barbecue Smokers Association
Bruce and Pam Paris
Carl Triola and Family
Carlene and Mitch Phelps (barbecuenews.com)
Captain BBQ
Carolyn and Gary Wells, Kansas City Barbecue Society
Charlie McMurry
Chris Sandberg
Christopher Ladner
Chuck Kruger, Entertainment Resources
Colette LeGrande
Cynthia J. Smith
Damnifino Team
Dan & Sue Brodsky

Daniel Ostroff
Dave DeWitt, *Fiery Foods* magazine
David Klose
David Skinner, Whirlpool Corporation
David and Mary Spriggs (newbookscheap.com)
Dean Dirks
Diana and Tom Dillard
Diana Loesch, Sow Luau
Diane Hampton and Lynn Doyle, Memphis in May
Delores Spruell-Jackson
Donna Myers, Hearth, Patio & Barbecue Association
Doug Fisher
Doug and Joyce Spittler
Doug Mosley, National Barbecue News
Duane Trygg
Ed and Julie Niland
Erin Kirk
Esther Lippman and Susanna Clyde

Fran Hall, Columbus Pig Jig
Frank Boyer, California Barbecue Association
Garry Howard, The Smoke Ring
Georgie Boy: Patrick Terveer, Rich Allen, Dick Yost, Jerry Dunfee, and Frank Long
Grant and June Browne
Grill to Go Team
Harry Aldrich, Oregon Cedar Grill Company
Hayward and Eva Harris, The Rib Doctor
Heather Bryan, Oregon Spices
Helen Himple, Travel Meetings & Incentives
Jack Bettridge and family
Jack Rogers, Jim Minion, The Car Dogs, Puyallup, Washington
Jamie Gwen, chef, Smart & Final
Jamieson Fuller
Jason Gronlund, chef, McIlhenny Company
Jeff Loya, Phil's BBQ
Jeff Miller, Vancouver Police Department, Vancouver, Washington
Jennie Halfant
Jennifer Alexander
Jennifer Lyons
JoAnn and Larry Laney
Joel Schroeder
John and Kathy Angood
John Davis
John Scroggins, Noble Communications
Jon and Jana Trueb, J & J BBQ, West Linn, Oregon
Judith Regan, ReganBooks
Kathleen S. Davis, Blue Mountain Design Works
Karen Adler, Pig Out Publications
Karen Gelbart, Food Network Canada
Karen Von Eisenburg, Bayer Corporation

KCTS-TV, Seattle: Jay Parikh, Randy Brinson, Glenn Dreyfuss, Greg Davis, Tim Olson, Tom Speer, Marion Smith, David Rabbinovich, Tom Niemi, Jeff Gentes, Erin Miller, Rupert Macnee, Curt Weiss, Noah Lehman
Lee McWright, Music City Pig Pals
Lisa Moore
Lou Brancaccio and family
Lynn and Jeff Shivers, IBCA
Kevin, Mary, Amber, and Stephen
Kevin Flannery, NEBS
Kurt Andrews, ReganBooks
Kyle Greenwood
Linda Myers, MYCOMM
Luther Echols' Club Red Team, Columbus, Georgia
Lynne Tolley, Miss Mary Bobo's
Mad Momma and the Kids
Marianne Beckwith
Marsha and Russ Matta, and the original Baxter
Melanie Jones
Michael Coyne
Mike & Ed's Barbecue, Phenix City, Arkansas
Miss Mary Bobo, Miss Mary Bobo's Boarding House
Misty River Band
Nathan Wu and Karen Kulm
Nick Spinelli Jr., Kraft Foods
Oliver Gomes
Patrick Faulstitch
Pat and Tara Bennett
Patti Abel, Work Kitchen Inc.
Patty Boday, Oregon Spice Company
Paul Kirk, the Baron of Barbecue
Peggy Scott
Phil Pace, Phil's BBQ
Regis Philbin
Randall Oliver, Smart and Final
Rhoda Varley and family
Rick and Barbara Smith
Rocky Danner, National Barbecue News
Rolf Zubler, World BBQ Association

Rose Arceneaux
Rubie Lloyd, ChefWear
Scott Campbell and family
Scott Ressmeyer, Country's, Columbus, Georgia
Smoke Stack Lightning
Sow Luau Team
Spats & Spoons Browne
Stephanie Wilson, KCBS
Steve Liberty, Trade Winds Motor Inn
Swine & Dine Team, Memphis, Tennessee
Swine Fellows Team
Tana Shupe, Jack Daniel's World Invitational
The Brownes: Kathy, Kara, Tricia and Chris
The Columbian Photogs: Milan Chuckovich, Kim Blau, Jerry Coughlan, Troy Wayrynen, Linda Lutes, Dave Olson, Janet L. Mathews, and Steve Lane
The Parikhs: Monica, Andrew, Jacob, and Rebecca
The Smiths: Barb, Jim, Abby, Anthony, Tyler, and Betsy
Thomas Sandmeier, Swiss Barbecue Artists
Tia Burke, The Rivermark, Memphis, Tennessee
Tiffany Collins, Houston Livestock Show
Tom and Charlie Vergos, The Rendezvous, Memphis, Tennessee
Tom Ryll
Tom Spear, Este's Men's Clothing, Portland, Oregon
Tony Spear, Este's Men's Clothing
Top Gun Brisketeers
Tracy Satterfield, American Royal
Valerie Schmid, Swiss Barbecue Artists
Virginia Peebles, Historic Columbus Foundation
Zoe Miller, Oregon Spice Company

Index